Praise

'A thoughtful, considered guide for leaders navigating this new epoch where human complexity meets accelerating technological change. What makes this book thoroughly engaging is the way Katie blends ideas from science, art, business and systems theory with psychoanalytic insight and vivid examples from her experience of leading in highstakes military environments. She normalises our messy human paradoxes and captures how fear can take hold and drive us into irrational group behaviour, when what we most need are leaders who can anchor groups and foster collective sensemaking. I found it a much-needed invitation to slow down and reconnect with the innate human capacities that can steady us in the uncharted waters of AI. This book offers practical, grounded steps to help leaders stay connected, curious and able to think clearly through uncertainty.'

— **Jennie McShannon**, Consultancy,
Facilitation, Team Coaching,
EMCC Senior Practitioner and Supervisor

'Katie Muldoon captures the defining paradox of our era: AI gives us unprecedented efficiency, but at the cost of the cognitive discomfort required for genuine growth. *Mind Your Self* moves past the superficial hype to address the true issue facing modern leaders – preventing our teams from using AI to "evacuate" the struggle of deep thinking. An essential, deeply perceptive guide for the future of leadership.'

— **Rob Stemp**, CTO DeepMinds Ltd

Mind Your Self

How **leaders** can integrate **AI** without disintegrating humans

KATIE MULDOON

Rethink | Press
PART OF ADVANTAGE | THE AUTHORITY COMPANY

First published in Great Britain in 2026
by Rethink Press (www.rethinkpress.com)

Published by Rethink Press, Norfolk, UK. An imprint of Advantage Media.

Rethink Press is an imprint of Advantage Media Group. Advantage Media helps busy entrepreneurs, CEOs, and leaders write and publish a book to grow their business and become the authority in their field. Advantage authors comprise an exclusive community of industry professionals, idea-makers and thought leaders. For more information go to advantagemedia.com.

Cover image © individual elements from unsplash.com and photo by Shyam on Unsplash

For B.H.
Thank you

Contents

Foreword

This is a strikingly assured book, and a timely one. At a moment when artificial intelligence is too often discussed either in the breathless language of salvation or the lurid vocabulary of catastrophe, this work offers something rarer and more useful: judgement.

On the surface this is about consequential decision-making in an AI environment, but its deeper concern is leadership itself. The author writes with an evident understanding of what it means to carry responsibility for others, to make decisions under pressure, to sustain trust, to preserve team cohesion and to remain clear-eyed when complexity threatens to overwhelm both process and instinct. Katie's observations on leadership are solidly underpinned by experience, but they are never self-regarding. Instead, they are used to illuminate a larger question: how can human beings think well, act safely and lead wisely when powerful new technologies enter the room?

One of the book's chief virtues is its balance. It is accessible without being simplistic, informed by neuroscience without becoming technical, and alert to the vulnerabilities of human cognition without lapsing into cynicism. The author is notably empathetic about our limitations: our biases, our fatigue, our need for trust and meaning within groups. Yet this is not an antitechnology tract. On the contrary, it is curious and hopeful about AI, seeing it not as a replacement for the sophisticated human brain, but as a tool that may sharpen, support and extend it when used with discipline.

The result is a readable, intelligent and quietly impressive contribution to one of the defining leadership questions of our age. Its argument is not that AI will make decisions for us, but that it will test the quality of the people and institutions using it. Those who care about judgement, responsibility and the human element in decision-making should read it with attention.

— **Major General (Ret'd) Sarah Johansen CB, MBE,**
former UK Deputy Chief Defence Intelligence

Introduction

In the middle of September 1941, the physicists Heisenberg and Bohr took a walk in Copenhagen. Twenty years earlier, they had been student and professor. They had gone on to develop the foundations for quantum mechanics, with Heisenberg developing his uncertainty principle. On that September evening, however, the world had changed – unravelled. Now they were on opposite sides of the Second World War: Heisenberg working for the Reich, and Bohr, part-Jewish, living in occupied Denmark. That walk – or, more precisely, that talk – is one of the great mysteries of scientific morality.

Heisenberg later claimed that he had been trying to warn Bohr of the intention Germany had and the progress it had made towards building an atomic bomb. He shape that direction directly, while most of us will be living in response to it. All of us, however, need to know ourselves in relation to AI – both what we think about it and who we are.

Responding with skill to AI is a task that all of us face. For those of us in leadership positions, the responsibility is acute. Doing it well will call for careful, deliberate thought about where and how we use it – and where and how we don't. Done well, AI can support us in spending more time, and applying more skill, to cultivating the things that truly make us human. Done clumsily, we may erode the very things that make us who we are.

Why did I write this book?

I wrote this book because my combination of experience kept returning me to the question of how to live and lead well alongside this new technology. An engineer by training, I served as an officer in the RAF for ten years, including three tours of duty in Afghanistan. After leaving the RAF, I worked initially in consulting and then in innovation and technology, relishing the power of bringing new technologies to the missions of government. Alongside this, I trained in Jungian psychoanalysis, exploring what truly makes us human and how we develop. From this, I developed my leadership practice, where I deliver psychodynamic executive education alongside my tech portfolio.

My time in the RAF taught me a lot about leadership at the edge. Facing the very real threat in Afghanistan, and leading people in that environment, honed my understanding of the irreducible core of what it means to be human: when we face moments of existential question, who are we? In the RAF and through the rest of my career, I have been a devotee of technology and what it can bring to us – from safer aviation through to time saved that I can reinvest with my loved ones. In my psychodynamic training, I have knitted both of those things together with a curiosity for, and reverence towards, the arts and humanity, which has upended, matured and refined how I think.

Using those three lenses to think about AI – and what being a leader in an age of AI means – shone a light on the challenge. If we use AI carefully and deliberately, preserving the best of what it means to be human alongside the technological advantages it brings, there is a bright future. If we are careless or inattentive, AI can easily strip out the developmental pathways on which our institutions rely, while corroding our specialist practitioners' ability to do their jobs. It's all there in the early research.

That's why I wrote this book. Most of us aren't Heisenberg or Bohr in this story, but all of us have a community – if not a nation – who could be relying on us for our consideration, our deliberate choices and our attentiveness to this most important moment.

In this book, you will find an exploration of how AI is interacting with human development, what that could look like in your workforce and the challenges it will bring. It has practical strategies to explore and understand this, and to develop you as the leader your institution and your community deserve. It is built on a career of service, and it is my deepest wish that it serves you as you step into the changing challenge of leadership in an AI world.

PART ONE
HOW DID WE GET HERE?

ONE

The Optimisation Trap: When Data Obscures Humanity

There is a clear, crisp vision of how AI could work in professional settings. It can remove the boring, monotonous tasks that take up so much of our time at work, freeing up time for us to be creative and focus on the harder end of problems that require original thought. It is already becoming established doctrine that there are crucial tasks and responsibilities where AI will require a human in the loop – tasks that are particularly complex, high stakes or need human connection. This vision creates a more meaningful experience at work and in life. We are spending more time on the core business of being human and potentially have more time with our loved ones or in our chosen pursuits.

Here's the paradox and the reason for this book: unless we are deliberate and careful in the way we use

AI, it can erode our ability to be that top-tier human thinker, doing the things that only humans can. Just as AI comes along promising more time for the strategic and creative problems you struggle to get to, it can also rob you of your ability to tackle them. This isn't great for AI, either. Good outcomes for AI will often depend on the human–AI partnership, but without being very deliberate, partnering with AI may erode your ability to be the human end of that partnership.

Integrating AI is a tightrope walk, with a significant fall at stake. Make it across the chasm and we'll find the potential to lean into our unique, embodied, creative selves. Misstep and we might lose the gamble – and our ability to think as well as we could.

The Zeigarnik experiment

Every person and every business or institution will need to respond to this – or is, in fact, already responding. Taking the time to explore what we know about how AI might disrupt how we develop and think, and choosing strategies to navigate that, will create a competitive edge for you and your work. This involves diving into some neurobiology, some development theory and some lessons about leadership. It also involves stories. Let's start with one that begins in a cafe a hundred years ago.

Picture a Berlin cafe in 1927. A group of university students and professors settle into their seats. The waiter takes order after order, without writing a single thing down. Impressed, the group returns to their conversation. After a short wait, every diner receives exactly what they ordered. The waiter's memory seems extraordinary.

After dinner, one of the students – a young Lithuanian-Soviet psychologist named Bluma Zeigarnik – realises she's left her scarf behind. She returns to find the waiter with the extraordinary memory and asks if he's seen it. He stares at her blankly. He has no idea who she is or where she sat.

'How can you have forgotten?' she asks, incredulous. 'Especially with your incredible memory!'

The waiter's reply is curt: 'I keep every order in my head until it is served.'

This simple exchange unlocked something profound about how human minds work, and decades later, it helps to explain why artificial intelligence might be quietly eroding our capacity to think.

Intrigued by the waiter's selective memory, Bluma Zeigarnik designed an experiment. She asked participants to complete simple tasks: solving puzzles, creating figures with clay, assembling flat-pack boxes. She interrupted them during about half of the tasks; the others were completed undisturbed.

She then asked participants to recall details about what they'd done. The results were striking: people remembered interrupted tasks about 90% better than completed ones.[2] The explanation lies in psychological tension. An unfinished task creates cognitive tension that keeps information accessible in memory. Completion releases that tension, allowing the brain to discard the details. The waiter's orders lived vividly in his mind until they were served, then his brain erased them to make room for new tasks.

The interplay between the brain's three core networks

What's going on in our brains that allows us to dismiss tasks once they are complete? It's an interplay between three core networks that coordinate how we think and feel. Each one has a different job:

1. **The Central Executive Network (CEN)** – as your task-focused brain – handles working memory, attention and executive functions when you're actively solving problems. I imagine I can feel this one firing when I hurtle through a busy workday.
2. **The Default Mode Network (DMN)** – as your reflective brain – activates when you're daydreaming, remembering the past, imagining the future and thinking about yourself and others. That's where you ponder, think more deeply and generate creative, complex solutions.

3. **The Salience Network (SN)** – as a switch in your brain – determines when you focus outwards on tasks and when you turn inwards for reflection. I imagine it as an old-fashioned railway signalman, switching the tracks for my mind to run along depending on the desired destination.

These three networks work together – although not always at the same time – to create the high-level thinking and emotional behaviours that make us human. Critically, the CEN and DMN are typically anticorrelated: when one turns on, the other turns off.

How AI causes cognitive debt

Keep these networks in mind as we jump to 2025. A study from MIT[3] goes viral with an alarming headline in *The Telegraph*: 'Using AI makes you stupid.'[4] The research reveals something crucial about what happens when we use AI through prompts. When we ask AI to complete a task for us, the CEN of the brain treats it as complete immediately. The brain's executive network concludes its work the moment the AI generates a response. Here's the critical part: the railway signalman of the SN never switches up the tracks to involve the deeper thinking network. The task never passes over to the DMN for deeper processing – for pondering, wondering, integrating with existing knowledge or making meaning.

MIT researchers found that students using ChatGPT displayed significantly reduced brain activity in areas linked to attention, memory and advanced reasoning compared to those who wrote independently or used search engines. More concerning, those who had used AI performed worse on subsequent tasks and struggled when asked to work without it. The researchers introduced the term 'cognitive debt' to describe the cumulative toll: similar to how using satnav has eroded our sense of direction. Cognitive debt is akin to 'technical debt' in software engineering: there is a short-term gain but a hidden liability is created. In this case, you get an easier and quicker answer, but long term you are losing your mental fitness to think critically, meaning that you will need to put in more effort to recover that lost cognitive ground.

A separate study from the University of Pennsylvania, involving over 4,500 participants, found that those who used ChatGPT to research topics 'developed shallower knowledge' than those using Google Search.[5] Their knowledge was less invested, sparser and not as original – precisely because the information synthesis was done for them rather than actively constructed through their own cognitive effort.

The waiter in that Berlin cafe forgot the orders once served. We forget our thinking once AI completes the task.

This is just one of the ways that using AI can impact our thinking; one of the examples of the paradox: while

AI could set us free to spend more time on human thinking, along the way it might reduce our capacity to do so. In the coming chapters, we will explore other ways it interferes with the way we think, develop and interact.

The machine that changed everything

Facing a moment in which technology disrupts a pattern of skills and knowledge and changes human society is far from new. There is a wealth of examples – many bringing fantastic progress – but they are nuanced and have profoundly impacted our experience of work.

In 1803, the poet Dorothy Wordsworth, sister of William Wordsworth, encountered a steam-powered water pump for the first time. She wrote in her journal: 'It was impossible not to invest the machine with some faculty of intellect; it seemed to have made the first step from brute matter to life and purpose.'[6]

She was witnessing the dawn of something momentous. Within decades, 'self-acting' machines, powered by steam and later electricity, would spread across Britain and beyond, 'accomplishing tasks once done only by human hands'.[7] The spinning jenny used eight spindles powered by a single wheel, allowing one spinster to produce eight threads in the time it had previously taken to make one. The cotton gin increased the productivity of removing seed from cotton at an incredible rate. What had taken skilled artisans hours now took minutes. Artisans and skilled workers were displaced. The factory was here to stay.

Something else happened, too – something darker that Dorothy Wordsworth couldn't have foreseen. As machines multiplied, the logic that governed them began to govern the people who worked alongside them. Humans were measured by the same metrics as machines: output per hour, efficiency, productivity. We were reduced to interchangeable parts in an increasingly mechanised system. By 1833, conditions had become so dire – particularly for children working long hours in dangerous factories – that parliament passed the Factory Act to impose basic protections,[8] but the psychological damage was already done.

For over two centuries, Western industrialisation has systematically reduced human work to measurable outputs and efficiency metrics, transforming people into machine components: predictable, quantifiable, optimised – and, in the process, measurably miserable. Now artificial intelligence arrives, promising to automate tasks and assist us in others, freeing us for more meaningful work.

We stand at a threshold: an opportunity to reclaim work as a space for meaning-making, growth and mature adult development. The catch is, even in early research, AI is showing itself to disrupt the foundations of our thinking, and history shows us it is far from inevitable that we know how to integrate new technologies in ways that enhance human life and work. It can be done (look at the myriad medical and civil engineering breakthroughs), but it isn't certain. When it comes to digital technology, success seems to be accompanied with cognitive risks.

The dopamine trap

More recently, digital technologies have been hijacking our attention and disrupting our thinking. In 2025, Tim Berners-Lee, the man who invented the World Wide Web, is watching his creation with growing alarm. He writes in his book *This Is for Everyone* that what is causing him alarm is the shift from the internet being an 'intention economy' to an 'attention economy'.[9] The algorithms are designed not to serve our intentions but to capture and hold our attention, exploiting a fundamental vulnerability in how our brains work.

Here's the vulnerability: we watch far more than we read, and this is a dopamine trick, a form of addiction. Our brains respond more readily to visual and auditory stimulation than to the effortful work of reading and imagining. It's the path of least resistance, and the algorithms know it.

When you read a book, your brain has to work. You encounter the sentence, 'it was dark, the rain tapped against the window, the panes shook with the wind' and your mind constructs the image: the weathered window, the fragile panes, the windy night. You're actively creating mental imagery, engaging multiple sensory systems beyond just vision. You're imagining.

When you watch that same window on a screen, the work is done for you: the images are given, pre-made, requiring no imaginative effort. Here's where it gets troubling: researchers at the University of York found that after people watched film clips, they displayed impaired imaginative capabilities for periods afterwards; they were slower at mental visualisation tasks compared to those who had been reading. While the immediate effect measured only 25 seconds, the researchers emphasise the cumulative impact: 'If you look at what this means over a longer period of time, days or years of consistently consuming images on screen, then we can see that this is actually a significant impact on the brain's ability to mentally visualise and feel.'[10]

Your imaginative muscles atrophy from disuse.[11] Imagination isn't just about conjuring images; it is how we consider someone – or something – other than ourselves, and how we recognise that others may have completely different ideas or experiences. It's the foundation of empathy, creativity and our capacity to envision alternative futures.

The erosion of our cognitive capacities through digital tech is an established phenomenon and we are layering AI on top of this, bringing even greater risk of cognitive atrophy. This is an urgent challenge professionally, but the opportunity is also real. There is a chance to build a competitive edge if you can protect your human capital while skilfully introducing AI.

The opportunity we might squander

AI genuinely offers the promise to automate tasks that should be automated: the repetitive, the mundane, the purely mechanical. This could free human capacity for what industrialisation suppressed: work that allows meaning-making, growth and development towards mature adulthood. Emotional maturity in the workplace – characterised by empathy, acceptance of responsibility, openness to feedback and learning, and adaptation to change – enables not just professional success but a natural maturation for the human mind. Through work experiences, we can progress through increasingly sophisticated levels of thinking and meaning-making.

Meaning-making is taking in everything in your experience and creating a way of working with it. It is how you make sense of what is happening – the story you tell yourself about it – and that underpins how you choose to move forwards. For example, if a colleague at work gives you some blunt feedback, the words are part of your experience but so too are the tone of voice, the environment you are in, your physiological response and how it connects to the broader context of your work and organisation. All of this is drawn on when you gather meaning from it and tell yourself a story about what happened to understand it. That story might range from 'that was helpful', to 'I need to pull my socks up', to 'I must not trust her'.

Your experience shapes your beliefs, and your beliefs determine your actions. How you process your experience is the meaning-making.

Will all this free time create a utopia of healthy workplaces and happy homes? Not if we remain increasingly overwhelmed by passive information that numbs us into long periods of watching. Not if our attention continues to be pulled away from intention. Not if we allow our imaginative, empathetic and abstractly reasoning neocortex to atrophy from disuse.

Your first task as a leader, as a professional and as a person is simple, if not easy, and by picking up this book you are already doing it. It is to engage, to enquire, to sit with the discomfort of the challenge – to seek it out and to explore the risks of the technology alongside its potential. It is to dive into understanding how we develop and think, at least enough to think through what this moment means for you, your team and your work. There will be some specific suggestions in the following chapters, but your first task is simply to read on.

TWO
The Execution Gap

The most essential growth that we experience is rooted in discomfort – sometimes deep discomfort. The times that have most shaped my own leadership and outlook, and driven me to develop and grow, have been rooted in deep discomfort. I would like to share one that shaped me the most: a short, sharp shock of a moment in the middle of Helmand Province, Afghanistan.

I was leading a team of helicopter engineers responsible for preparing and launching aircraft for a range of missions, including medical evacuation. We were doing scheduled maintenance work in the hangar when the aircrew for a medical evacuation came running in, heading straight towards me to find out which helicopters were ready and could fly, *now*.

Minutes matter – there was an injured soldier out there, and getting this crew to him now would make the difference.

We had trained for this moment – every cell in our bodies had been trained for this moment. The preparation was excellent, the equipment was ready, we were in position. The window of opportunity was open – not wide, but open. We had a crucial 'golden hour' to rescue an injured soldier.

I watched it happen in the Afghan dust, my eyes darting to each of the team members with each breath I took. They were ready; some poised in race positions like F1 pit-crew members. I was running through the scenario perfectly, but between intention and action, something had severed. An invisible gap had opened, and the team was suspended across it, capable of everything except the one thing that mattered: execution.

They weren't frozen with fear. They were paralysed by possibility. The helicopter wasn't working and we had moments to sort it out. The rotors had not started turning. The pilots looked up and down, left and right, arms up, turning switches on and off. Some of my team scrambled over the helicopter desperately searching for what had broken. Some stared, frozen, dropping tools and spilling oil. Others began to cry.

I watched the timer. It was over, too late. I called it in, we couldn't do it. We had to turn to the stand-by helicopter in another detachment. Our medical evacuation crew and my engineers remained on the ground, unable to undertake the most important mission: rescuing a comrade. We were absolutely devastated.

This was the moment that changed my understanding of leadership forever. Not the moment weeks later when we were reliably making it through, but this moment when I realised that the distance between knowing and doing isn't measured in metres or minutes; it's measured in psychological space – in the liminal void between who we are and who we must become to act.

In the weeks and months that followed, I learnt a lot about how to cross that gap. It is called the execution gap. Crossing it requires grit, discomfort and learning through experience. You will be able to call to mind your own examples where you learnt to master something crucial through sustained effort. The challenge with AI, as we will see, is that it removes much of that discomfort. It removes the requirement for grit.

Designing AI to preserve the grit

If we carefully design the how, when and where of bringing AI into our personal and professional lives, we can make deliberate choices about where we want to remove that grit. We can also carefully design how to protect the spaces where we need to preserve the grit and discomfort of crossing the execution gap for ourselves. We need a flourishing partnership between ourselves and AI, which means making sure we can bring all the human skill we have to that partnership.

If we don't carefully design how we use AI, the temptation to avoid the discomfort and grit may prove a little too great. Sure, AI can cross the chasm of the execution gap for you. The problem is this: if you rely on AI in the wrong way, when you really need to cross it as a human, you are out of practice.

Imagine you are learning a language. You can ask a large language model (LLM) to do your translation homework for you and you'll get a perfect score, but you are not crossing the gap yourself. When you find yourself on holiday, eager to ask for directions or chat with the locals, there is no bridge – no stepping stones – to do it.

We can grasp that so easily for learning a language, but there are many ways in which the temptation to leave the execution gap to AI could erode your overall ability to perform the important human parts of your life and work.

Why is this skill so important – so critical to being human? The clearest example is perhaps the simplest: a toddler reaching for a toy just beyond their grasp.

Ego strength and optimal frustration

Watch that child. They stretch, strain and fail. They try again. Their face contorts with effort. Perhaps they cry in frustration. Through this utterly necessary struggle, something extraordinary happens in their developing brain: neural pathways strengthen. The hippocampus encodes memories of challenge and triumph, the prefrontal cortex learns to persist despite discomfort, and, most crucially, something called ego strength begins to build.

Ego strength is not arrogance or aggression. It's the psychological capacity to tolerate discomfort, maintain purpose in the face of obstacles, and act despite doubt. Children who experience manageable adversity within supportive relationships develop resilience – the neural and psychological architecture that allows them to weather life's gaps and uncertainties.

The key word is manageable. 'Optimal frustration', psychoanalysts call it. Struggle that's bearable. Failure that happens within the container of a reliable relationship. That's the blueprint of how to develop and grow, both as a human and as a leader. We see it most clearly in our youngest children, but it remains an ongoing task. You probably have a project you are engaged in right now where optimal frustration is helping you learn and grow. It might be a hobby, such as knitting, or a new work challenge, such as developing a new system for your team, but you can probably conjure exactly how it feels. Keep that feeling in mind. It is your competitive edge, and I don't want you to lose it – or the ability to tolerate it – when AI offers you an endless array of easier options.

The importance of human connection

Imagine your interactions with AI so far. It responds instantly, perfectly attuned to your emotional state. It never judges, never disappoints, never requires the difficult work of 'rupture and repair' that characterises genuine human relationships, skill-building and real resilience. Not only does it not require you to master the associated skills, but it also makes no demands on your skills to interact well with others. It is brilliant, efficient, uncanny.

Psychological research reveals something troubling about that last point – human connection. While AI companions temporarily reduce loneliness by creating the feeling of being heard, heavy reliance on them correlates with greater isolation and reduced motivation to seek human connection. AI provides a perfectly responsive mirror, reflecting back only what we wish to see and never challenging us to grow.

In our effort to protect people from struggle, we have accidentally destroyed their capacity for execution.

Let's stick with the importance of human connection for a minute. It is vital to your leadership, and it is one of the things that AI could erode if you let it. There is an important concept from early years development called attunement, which describes how parents respond to their child's needs. There is also a completely counterintuitive finding that discovered that 'perfect attunement' – every need met, every communication understood – can actually impair a child's development.[12]

Apart from relieving you of some parental guilt, this insight shines a light on the importance of grit and discomfort to being human. We need to know that our parents are fallible and make mistakes but that they keep trying to understand. The child, in turn, must learn that they can withstand things not going perfectly.

This rupture-and-repair cycle does something remarkable to the developing brain. It teaches the child that disconnection is survivable. That relationships can withstand discord. That conflict doesn't destroy connection but can deepen it. These experiences literally wire the neural capacity for resilience – the ability to maintain emotional balance and purposeful action in the face of uncertainty.

AI interaction offers none of this developmental crucible. It provides consistency without challenge, validation without the discomfort that prompts growth. It builds no backbone into the experience of relationships. The result? A population standing at the execution gap with no training in crossing it.

The good news is: you don't have to be among this population. You can lead in a way that prevents your team and your organisation from risking this, too. It's not easy – of course it isn't – but given how much I've hammered on about grit and discomfort, you didn't expect it to be, did you?

The bridge exists

Let me tell you how I got the team in Afghanistan to move into action. I reached for a classic. Not the *Odyssey* on this occasion, nor even Sun Tzu's *The Art of War*. This time, as I lay in the dust, all I could think about was... Indiana Jones

Indy stands at a precipice. His father is dying. The Holy Grail, which might save him, lies across a chasm. The instruction is cryptic: 'Only in the leap from the lion's head will he prove his worth.'[13] He cannot see the path. Every sensory input screams that stepping forward means death. Yet he places his hand over his heart, closes his eyes and steps into the apparent void. His foot lands on solid stone. The camera shifts, revealing what was always there: a bridge perfectly camouflaged against the far wall. From one perspective, emptiness. From another, a solid path.

This is the execution gap made visible.

The bridge exists. It has always existed. Until we commit to the step – until we move through that liminal space with faith in something beyond what we can currently perceive – we remain trapped on the safe side of potential.

As I looked from crestfallen face to crestfallen face, I knew I had to be the team's bridge. This was execution paralysis. The team standing at the edge isn't lazy, fearful or uncommitted. They were standing at a developmental threshold – and they couldn't cross it alone. To build that bridge I had to think about attunement, narrative and agency.

Attunement

We talked about attunement earlier in this chapter, so you already know it doesn't have to be perfect, but if you are guiding a team over that execution gap, they need to be seen, heard and understood. They need to know they aren't alone.

When we failed to get that helicopter out and a Chinook from another squadron was sent instead, I knew I needed to switch up how I was leading. Two very young members of my squadron were deeply distressed by our failure in the moment. We sat together, and I let them know that I had seen their commitment and their courage, even if we hadn't succeeded this time. This let them know that they were seen and I was paying attention to how they felt inside.

On a scientific note, this sense of being seen and understood by someone else quite literally regulates your nervous system, moving you out of a shut-down state and into one where thinking and execution become possible again.

For you as a leader, the key is to tune into what is happening – in the room, in the meeting, in the team. Make observations and ask questions about what is going on for people. Remember, you don't have to get this perfectly right. What makes it work isn't your ability to guess what people are feeling but the simple act of enquiry and paying attention. Don't try and change what they are feeling or explain facts about the situation. Just enquire, sit with them and pay attention. You are attuning. It has a magic of its own in helping people move back into execution.

We all need to feel understood and to experience trusted relationships with others. This doesn't mean perfect understanding. It means the sustained effort to perceive another's internal state and respond in ways that communicate: 'I see you. I understand what you're facing. You're not alone.'

Neuroscientist Stephen Porges' Polyvagal Theory[14] suggests that this felt sense of being perceived and understood by another helps regulate our nervous system, moving us from defensive states into the ventral vagal zone, where exploration and execution become possible.

Narrative

We all need to make sense of the world and predict what may happen next. The human brain is a prediction machine, constantly attempting to minimise surprise and uncertainty. When we lack narrative coherence – when we cannot tell ourselves a story that makes sense of past, present and future – we become dysregulated.

After that failure in the team, I started to explore the story the team were telling themselves. Either they weren't telling one at all or they were telling themselves they were no good at their jobs – that what they did didn't matter. The challenge of our role was that it was a small piece in a much bigger operation. We had one clear task: to get the Merlin into the air at the moment it was needed. We had, however, lost sight of the bigger story: we were there to rescue our injured comrades. We knew this intellectually but we had stopped feeling it, and for a story to make sense, it needs heart.

I introduced an end-of-shift debrief. As well as reflecting on the good and bad of that shift, I used it to update the team on what had happened to the soldiers our Merlins had gone out to rescue. It was rarely a simple good news story – if you need an airlift out of Afghanistan, things have gone wrong – but the honesty in the updates, and the good news within them, gave a real, beating heart back to the team.

They heard stories of the injured who recovered – sometimes of those who wouldn't have made it, but did. When the stories were harder and people didn't make it, we at least knew that they would be returned to their families. Building those stories – both the uplifting ones and the ones that saddened us deeply – gave us a reason to keep crossing the threshold of the execution gap. We knew what meaningful stories lay on the other side.

When leaders help their teams construct meaning – when they provide a compelling story that explains why action matters and where it leads – they quite literally calm the threat-detection systems that trigger execution paralysis.

For you as a leader, have a think about what stories you are telling on purpose and when and where you are telling them. Connecting people to a meaningful purpose – to a story that they can understand and believe in – is key to helping them cross the execution gap. They need to know what story they will be able to tell on the other side. They need to know that the journey is worth the discomfort.

Agency

We all need to feel that we matter and that we can influence the course of our lives. Learnt helplessness – the psychological state Maier and Seligman discovered when organisms experience repeated uncontrollable stress – is the enemy of execution.[15] When people believe their actions have no consequence, the brain adapts by ceasing to initiate action. Agency is the antidote. It's built through repeated experiences of cause and effect: I act, something happens, my action mattered.

In Afghanistan, I shifted how I was leading. I moved from being the one issuing every instruction and order to the person setting out the intent while creating space in which people were authorised to operate independently. This gave them agency – a space to execute their expertise in service of the mission. I learnt a lot about letting the team have that space to operate. (Including the importance of having some fun along the way, but that is a story for Chapter 5.)

For you as a leader, where can you create opportunities for your team to exercise agency? Where can you provide space for their input, suggestions and ideas – and be willing to act on them? There will always be decisions that must remain with you, but where are the opportunities for you to set an intent and let your team stretch their wings a little? Where are you creating the chance for them to surprise you?

The extra dimension: The AI challenge

We've looked at just how critical crossing that execution gap is. We've reflected on why we get stuck and how to help get teams moving. We've touched on how AI can disrupt that, but I want to pause on that a little longer.

AI is a fantastic resource. I am a believer. I have integrated it into my workflows, I use it to help me get a grip of my tasks and I have even applied it to code an app to help me understand my tax, but it's a tool. Just as a blade can be used for surgery or violence, we need to make deliberate choices about when, where and why to use AI, and when, where and why *not* to.

AI removes friction – that is its selling point – but this whole chapter is about the power of friction. In fact, how essential it is to the development of healthy, creative human beings. We need to retain friction to remain human.

We know that trees grown in harsh elements create the strongest wood. We know that if you help a butterfly out of its chrysalis it won't develop the strength in its wings to fly. These are almost modern folk myths, but there is strong science behind them – and interesting emerging science, too. We need that friction to develop properly, and we need to keep exercising those muscles to retain them. That's the bad news: our need for struggle, for the grit and the discomfort, is never really over.

Stay with the struggle

This reminds me of that great line in *Julius Caesar*, where Caesar contemplates why he doesn't trust Cassius – and well he might, as Cassius is at the root of his ultimately fatal trouble. 'Cassius has a lean and hungry look; He thinks too much: such men are dangerous.'[16]

I am not advocating that you construct a complex plot leading to the death of Caesar – literally or metaphorically – but isn't there something in that 400-year-old phrase that serves us now? Don't overthrow the government, but... maybe... have a 'lean and hungry look'? Think, 'too much'. Be 'dangerous'. AI invites us to do the opposite – to become the men that Caesar wants about him, with discomfort and struggle removed and nothing to strive for. As Caesar says, 'Let me have men about me that are fat.'

When you begin to let AI take the discomfort away, as well as the inefficiency and the mundane, you erode your own expertise in crossing the execution gap. You outsource your creativity, your unanswered questions and your chance for growth. I am far from saying, 'Don't use AI!', but I do advocate for deliberate choice. How are you using it? How is it supporting your ability to get on in there, in the discomfort and the mess? Are you letting it assist you into the tricky questions, giving you just enough insight and information to step off that bridge and into the unknown, or are you letting it remove the need for that step altogether?

Ultimately, this is a deeply personal choice. What supports one person to stay with the discomfort may stop another from entering it. I invite you to do an honest AI audit, with the simple question: Is this helping me to stay with the discomfort, or offering me a pass so I don't have to experience it?

This invitation to stay with the struggle is crucial. Struggle is not a failure of the system; it *is* the system. The capacity to tolerate discomfort, to work through confusion, to sit with uncertainty until meaning emerges. This is not a failure of good design; this is the only way the human apparatus for thinking develops.

The promise of AI is to eliminate struggle. The danger is that, in doing so, it eliminates the very mechanism through which human beings develop the capacity to think, to grow, to mature. To become leaders. To become whole.

A wise leader in the age of AI will not be one who outsources thinking to machines. It will be one who insists on struggle, on difficulty, on the necessity of genuine relationships and encounters. It will be one who provides containment – the steady presence that allows people to remain in their window of tolerance while they do the genuine work of thinking, learning and becoming.

This leader will understand that their role is not to have all the answers. It is to create the psychological and relational conditions under which genuine thinking can occur. To absorb the anxiety of uncertainty. To model the capacity to think under pressure. To be changed by the people they lead. To hold the possibility that something new might emerge – something that neither the leader nor the led could have predicted, but that emerges from their genuine encounter with each other and with the complexity they face together.

This is not a return to the past. It is an insistence that the future must include what is most essentially human: the capacity to be with our own – and each other's – complexity, and to be transformed by that encounter. It is a defence of the irreducible value of struggle, of difficulty and of the human relationship as the ground of all genuine development and knowledge.

In an age that promises frictionless access to everything, the truly countercultural act is this: to insist that difficulty matters. That confusion, tolerated and worked through, is where growth lives. That genuine relationship – the kind that changes both people – is irreplaceable. That the container-contained relationship – whether between mother and infant, leader and team, or analyst and patient – remains the fundamental architecture through which human beings develop their capacity to think, to love, to become fully human.

Summary of the three approaches to crossing the execution gap, and why they matter

Approach	What it is	Why it matters	Example
Attunement	We all need to feel understood and to experience trusted relationships with others. This doesn't mean perfect understanding. It means the sustained effort to perceive another's internal state and respond in ways that communicate: 'I see you. I understand what you're facing. You're not alone.'	Being seen and understood by someone else quite literally regulates your nervous system, moving you out of a shut-down state and into one where thinking and execution become possible again.	After a high-stakes meeting, noticing that your team member is still stressed, taking the time to sit with them, have a cup of tea and talk it through, gives them the chance to regulate their nervous system with you, feel less alone and move into a more grounded state.

(Continued)

Approach	What it is	Why it matters	Example
Narrative	We all need to make sense of the world and anticipate what may happen next. The human brain is a prediction machine, constantly attempting to minimise surprise and uncertainty.	When we lack narrative coherence – when we cannot tell ourselves a story that makes sense of the past, present and future – we become dysregulated.	When facing a difficult deadline on a tricky project, the team comes together around the story that we have a great team with the right experience and skills to get this done, we will all stay on this until it is delivered and afterwards we will go out for a team celebration. This helps them acknowledge that it is hard right now but there will be a good outcome. They know through the narrative that it won't last forever.
Agency	We all need to feel that we matter and can influence the course of our lives.	When people believe their actions have no consequence, their brain adapts by ceasing to initiate action. Agency is the antidote. It's built through repeated experiences of cause and effect: I act, something happens, my action mattered.	You spot an issue at work. When you feel a sense of agency, you bring an energy, conviction and tenacity to raising and resolving it. Without that, you would probably just walk past it.

THREE

We Think Together

In Chapter 2 we explored the execution gap – how AI can make it harder to cross and how good leadership builds a bridge. A key idea was that discomfort is not only survivable but essential to building the grit and experience that makes us capable of crossing that gap. In this chapter, I am going to build on the idea that staying with this discomfort is crucial to developing and maintaining our human capacities. This time, it is not just about the ability to cross the execution gap – to *do* – but about our ability to *think*.

It turns out that thinking is not a lone sport, despite our idea of the noble genius, ensconced in an ivory tower, thinking great thoughts and disseminating them into the world. That is an illusion. Thinking is a team sport.

Developing the capacity to think together

Let's start at the beginning – back to infancy – where the foundations of our experiences are laid down and the pattern is sometimes easier to see.

Imagine a baby, a few months old. She is hungry. Her stomach hurts with the sharp, intolerable presence of hunger that is, to her, the end of the world. There is no past, no future – only this moment of complete and incomprehensible suffering. She cries.

Her mother hears. She does not panic. She does not rush in, saying, 'Stop suffering, I have the answer.' She does something simpler. She comes. She picks up her baby. Her nervous system is calm, even as her baby's is on fire. She holds the child, and her calmness begins to move into the baby. This is attunement, just as we discussed in Chapter 2. 'There, there,' she says. 'I know it hurts. I'm here.' Her voice has a particular quality – not the frantic tone of someone who cannot tolerate the baby's pain but the steady tone of someone who has seen suffering before and knows what happens next.

She feeds the baby. The milk comes. The pain subsides. The baby's nervous system gradually settles. The baby falls asleep.

This happens again tomorrow… and the next day… and the next.

What have we learnt? Not information. Not facts. Something stranger and more fundamental: the baby is learning that relief is possible after suffering. She is learning that her distress can be received by another mind without destroying that mind. She is learning – though she has no words for it yet – that her pain can be tolerated, metabolised, transformed by another person who loves her.

This is the beginning of what psychoanalysts call the 'capacity to think'. Not the capacity to know facts, but the capacity to hold an experience in mind without being destroyed by it. The mother is doing this first. She is doing the thinking for the baby. Gradually, through thousands of moments like this, the baby internalises the mother. She learns to do for herself what the mother has done for her.

You need discomfort to be able to learn to think... and you need other people. In this instance, it is the mother, but over time in our development that sequence, struggle, experience, finding our way through, gets repeated with different people: playmates, teachers, peers, colleagues.

To be able to endure this discomfort, we have to create a 'window of tolerance', as Dan Siegel describes it – neither overwhelmed (hyperarousal) nor shut down (hypoarousal).[17] The window of tolerance is the period of time during which we can experience that developmental struggle without it feeling overwhelming or impossible. We saw earlier how that begins at the start of life – the baby is beginning to build a sense of the window of tolerance: that she can endure discomfort and that relief will come. We have to continue to build that window and broaden it across all sorts of contexts if we want to keep developing.

One of my favourite psychoanalysts is Wilfred Bion. He worked with soldiers after the Second World War and became really interested in trying to understand the capacity to think. He argued that thinking wasn't a private, individual exercise (think back to that myth of the genius in the ivory tower), but something that we learn to do – and continue to do – together.[18] It is the presence of another human (or several) that allows you to explore concepts that, alone, you might merely experience. Think about that hungry baby, only experiencing discomfort until, with her mother, she is able to understand that these experiences happen but can be relieved.

Together, we learn to think about things. Together, we make meaning of our world. This requires discomfort – and other people.

We know that not everyone gets a great start in life. Modern psychology powerfully and sadly documents quite how important those first two years of life are, when this capacity to think together begins to emerge. If that process is disrupted, the child – and the adult they grow into – will work to recover and rectify it for the rest of their lives.

We also know that these fundamental dynamics show up at work. I am not asking you to parent your team at all, but to be a good leader you will need to help your team and your organisation learn how to think together.

Remaining within the window of tolerance under stress

A helicopter has crashed. I do not have the complete information. I do not know whether the crash was caused by enemy fire or by an accident. I do not know which of the three helicopters I signed as safe to fly has crashed. I know only that something has happened, and I must decide: in this moment, what do my troops need?

They need me not to panic. I must stay within my window of tolerance – the zone in which thinking is actually possible. If I move into hyperarousal, flooded with fear and pushed into fight-or-flight reactivity, then my cognitive function goes offline. My amygdala hijacks my prefrontal cortex. I will issue brittle, reactive, defensive orders. Conversely, if I shut down, freeze or become unable to act, that is equally catastrophic.

There are devices on the helicopter that must be recovered or destroyed due to the crash; the people will already have been evacuated. 'We can do this,' I say.

'The recovery team needs to get ready now. You've got this.'

What is happening here is not what many people might imagine command-and-control in the military is like. It is something else. It is containment. The regulatory function I offer the team allows them to remain in their window of tolerance. My calmness teaches them calmness. My capacity to tolerate uncertainty without rushing to premature decision-making gives them permission to do the same. I'm not saying, 'We have the answer.' I'm saying, 'We don't know yet, but I know how to be with not-knowing.'

That is how you think together. You start by showing people – through your reactions, your presence, your tone and your questions – that we can navigate this experience together, and once you have regulated together you can think together.

That team thought together. They spoke quicky but clearly, and assembled the kit and people that they would need to either salvage or destroy the sensitive kit on the crashed helicopter. They quietly boarded another helicopter and flew to the crash site, working through their options and ensuring no sensitive kit was left behind in a way that could do damage.

When people trust that their leader is containing the anxiety, that the boundaries are secure and that it is safe to not know temporarily, they become capable of innovation, of learning from experience, of noticing what is actually happening rather than what they expected to happen.

This is what successful military organisations have learnt through hard experience. The capacity to remain within the window of tolerance under extreme stress is exactly what a containing leader provides. I was, in that moment, serving the grown-up function for the troops that my mother once served for me as an infant. I was absorbing the shock of uncertainty and returning it in a form they could bear. I was demonstrating, through my presence and my steady voice, that uncertainty can be tolerated without destroying you. They, in turn, were able to think with me, to think with each other and to solve the problem.

The arrival of AI: Certainty without understanding

So far, so good. We need to think together, and good leaders understand that this is a team sport, but with the societal advent of AI, maintaining that capability in your team (which is already complex) is about to get harder. Why?

We've explored how important discomfort is in developing our capacity to think, but AI is beginning to provide an appealing way to sidestep that discomfort. AI offers the fantasy of something wonderful: immediate answers, frictionless knowledge and the elimination of the gap of not knowing.

When a leader faces an uncertain decision, they can query an AI and receive a confident-sounding recommendation. They do not have to tolerate the discomfort of not knowing; they do not have to sit with complexity and wait for clarity to emerge. The AI offers the illusion of certainty.

When a person faces emotional pain, they can ask an AI to help them process it. Here is what they cannot do: they cannot be witnessed. They cannot be received by another mind that is changed by encountering them because the AI has no mind to be changed. The AI may change the text it returns, but what AI returns is not knowledge but the appearance of another person's knowing, a code of what someone else knew rendered as language. It has no capacity for genuine relationship.

The person experiences the transaction as if it were authentic. This is the uncanny quality of AI. It mimics relationships so perfectly that we can almost believe the relationship is happening, like a child encountering a mirror for the first time, believing something alive lives in the glass.

The creative act – the living, struggling encounter between two minds, where something genuinely new can emerge – is absent. An AI cannot be psychologically changed by you. It cannot have its perspective transformed by your particular struggle. It cannot offer you the containing function because it has no psyche to be disturbed by yours.

The risk is not that AI provides information. Information is useful. The risk is that it provides information without the struggle and the partnership of others, which is how genuine thinking develops.

Bion coined a term for what happens when the apparatus for thinking is avoided or damaged: 'evacuation'.[19] Instead of thinking about their pain, a person simply gets rid of it. Instead of sitting with the discomfort of not knowing, they escape it. Over time, the capacity for genuine thinking atrophies.

What we risk creating, through the installation of AI as the universal problem-solver, is a society of people who have learnt to evacuate away from difficulty rather than to experience it. People who have the appearance of knowledge but not the underlying apparatus for generating it. People who can recite answers but have not thought.

Think about how that could show up in your life and your work. We know that the problems you are facing are likely to be novel and complex. They need genuine human creativity, spontaneity of thought – a group becoming more than the sum of its parts. These questions are for you, as both a user of AI and a leader of teams using it: How do I grow and maintain that capacity to think? What place can AI have in helping us with tasks and information? How do we make sure we don't let it erode our edge, our capacity to think together?

The questions that AI cannot answer

There is something else at stake here, something fundamental to human maturity: the loss of genuine relationship.

Knowledge is not a brick, an inert object that can be transferred from one mind to another. The creative act lies in the knowing – the encounter between two minds where something genuinely new emerges. If only one person knows, it remains a secret. We know from psychology what secrets do: they corrode, they fragment, they create shame and isolation.

When knowledge is generated only between you and an AI, something crucial is lost. The experience remains unwitnessed. It remains secret, and secrets poison the self.

In military leadership, trust is built not through commands or information but through presence. Through standing with people in uncertainty. Through being changed by what they contribute. Through the willingness to say, 'I don't know, and neither do you, but we can work this out together.' An algorithm cannot do this.

In education, learning is not the transfer of information – a function that AI can increasingly do better than humans can – but the development of the thinking apparatus itself. That apparatus develops only through an encounter with another mind that is genuinely present, genuinely challenged by the student's particular struggle and genuinely invested in their transformation.

If you want to keep yourself and your team thinking, you will need to be deliberate about the work that you do – and don't – bring AI in on. There isn't a fixed formula that can do the thinking for you on this one, and even if I cooked one up, by the time this book is published AI will have developed in new ways that outdate it.

There are some simple principles we can distil that can help us choose. Here are some questions to help you to make the deliberate choices about AI, to help you maintain discomfort and human connection where they are needed.

Is using AI here helping me to sidestep discomfort?

If it is, you might need to lean into the discomfort instead. You will need to be vigilant. You are a creative and canny creature, and you will find all sorts of ways to justify the use of AI: it is faster, better quality, more efficient. At the heart of it, only you can answer: Am I really using it to avoid feeling uncomfortable? If the answer is yes, you might need to do the thing yourself and lean into that discomfort.

Is using AI here putting me in contact with other people to think together or isolating me from them?

Not every use of AI will take you away from people. You might be using it to conduct a repetitive task you can do in your sleep, freeing up time to spend with your team. You might be using it to get ideas on how to plan a workshop or an offsite that will bring people together to think. You might also – if you interrogate your motives – find yourself using it instead of reaching out. Looking for an answer to something complex and novel that would be better explored with others. You might be turning to AI so you don't have to admit you don't know, or because doing the work with people feels vulnerable. Those are your warning signs.

Ultimately, only you can make these calls, but answering the above honestly should give you a solid grounding in whether this is something AI can help you with or whether you need to grab your team and think together.

As an example, I interviewed someone for my MBA thesis who was learning a language as a hobby. They had a strict set of rules about when they queried an LLM for help. They had to try and answer the question from memory first, then use their reference textbook, then a dictionary. If they were still struggling, they would take a break and try those steps again. Only then, if they still couldn't work it out, they would ask for help from an LLM. Even then, they made sure they understood the answer it gave before moving on. The individual said that the joy wasn't in the answer – the translation – but in coming to understand that language from the inside out, and to do that, they needed to slog through the hard bits. Otherwise, they might as well just read that language in translation. After all, every single thing they wanted to read already existed in translation in English. My interviewee hadn't dismissed the help of an LLM, but had found a way to use it as an aid to independence, not a crutch.

You might also need to create a team that can think together when they are facing one of those flight, fight or freeze moments I have told you about from my time in the military. That might be context-related, but increasingly – as AI pervades more and more of our personal and working lives – you might find yourself needing to get a team thinking that aren't doing that routinely anymore. Here are three questions to ask yourself as you diagnose the situation that can help you get your team thinking together. They come from both my psychoanalytic training and my experience in the military:

Can they think?

If they can, you should see someone in front of you who is calm and engaged. If instead you see someone who is frightened, mistrustful or frozen, they might not be able to think. Their nervous system has shifted into hyperarousal – fight or flight – where the amygdala has flooded the system with cortisol and adrenaline. The prefrontal cortex, where reasoning actually lives, has been partially taken offline by the emergency response system.

Think of a trauma survivor in the moment just after a triggering event, a soldier pinned down by fire, or an employee who has just been publicly humiliated. In this state, thinking is not available.

What do you do if your team is here? Appeals to logic won't work because logic is not available. What is available is reactivity, defensive posturing and hypervigilance.

Here is what you do: you offer safety, explicitly and repeatedly. This is an embodied action. Slow down your speech, lower the volume of your voice, make your movements deliberate and visible. Say clear, reassuring things: 'I see you. That was tough.' You are offering your own regulated nervous system to soothe theirs.

Are they wavering?

If the team before you are wavering, they are hovering in the difficult zone between hyperarousal (fighting) and collapse (inability to act). Their window for tolerating difficulty has become too narrow. One moment they are fighting, the next they are numb and disconnected. They might rage and then suddenly go silent. They might be hyperalert and then dissociate. (I have definitely been in team meetings like that. Those of you with teenagers at home will certainly recognise this state.)

With someone in this state, you need to do something a little different. You need to establish consistent boundaries and clearly name what is happening. You need to help put words to the feelings and sensations: 'I can see the range of emotions. That makes sense given what's happened. We can work this out together. We don't have to figure everything out right now, but we do need to stay present together.'

In a leadership context, this is less about soothing and more about steadiness. The message is this: you are safe not because I will eliminate all difficulty but because I will remain stable and present while you move through it. I will not abandon you. I will not panic with you.

Are they listening?

To think together, we need to be able to listen. When you have someone who is listening, they have a regulated nervous system and they will demonstrate both logical and operational thinking, processing facts and information and exploring them.

To test that, try to explore the topic with them. Get them talking. What do they think about the situation? What are their ideas? You aren't just initiating thinking here, you are also testing that they aren't caught in either of the two states above.

When we were dealing with that downed helicopter, I knew that the team moved into this phase when they started planning who needed to go and what kit they needed, and they began brainstorming scenarios and anticipating the problems they might face. They didn't actually need me at that point. They needed me as a leader in the moment before, when for a fraction of time they had frozen, not knowing how to move to the answers. Together, we regulated – together, we steadied – and at that point, they were thinking once more as a team to solve a difficult situation.

Using AI in the right way

Leadership is never easy, and navigating a world in which you and your employees will be the first tranche of people integrating AI into work adds a difficulty score that you probably wouldn't have chosen. As this chapter shows, it can also get us to explore what really makes us human, what makes us excellent and to find ways to protect that from erosion.

If we play this right, we can also choose how, when and where we use AI to create more time to do those things together as a team. If we integrate AI in the right way, in the right places, we can put human thinking on the challenges that really matter at work, but it won't happen organically. We need to fight our own instincts and explore how to do that. We need to think together.

PART TWO

HOW WILL LEADERSHIP NEED TO ADAPT?

FOUR

The Human In The Loop

If you are a UK reader, there is a fairly good chance you will remember a government advert showing a ballet dancer lacing up her pointe shoes, with the caption: 'Fatima's next job could be in cyber (she just doesn't know it yet).'[20] It caused an absolute furore and had to be shelved, with critics pointing out the insensitivity of the timing as so many arts jobs were being lost during the pandemic. It also spoke to something deeper – something more powerful than just insensitive timing. The real hope of what technology can do in our world is that it gives us more time to do the things that only humans can do. This advert, which sought to divert Fatima from her dancing career to one in cyber security, taps into a deeper fear: that technology will make us more like it, rather than it giving us more time to become ourselves.

The human–AI partnership

We have some big, pressing questions to ask ourselves about where we want AI to fit into our personal and professional lives. There is every chance that you are wrestling with these in a work context. What can AI do, and what should it do? Where can we safely replace human work with this new kind of machine? How do we make sure that the humans can still do the human part?

These aren't entirely new questions. Have you ever commented that a pilot landed a plane smoothly? Or have you ever smiled wryly, said 'that was a bit bumpy!', and assumed that the pilot was having a bad day on a less-than-perfect touch-down? Chances are that software delivered that light-as-a-feather landing and your slightly rough-around-the-edges one was the human effort. Aviation has been figuring out where and when you use automation and where and when you need humans for decades.

Flying planes is largely an automated job now. The sophistication of the aircraft and the operating systems is such that the machines do a better and safer job than unassisted humans could. The aviation industry, however, realised that passengers want a human at the front. They need to believe that there is someone flying – and landing – the plane; someone with a smart hat and wings above their heart. Getting on a plane and flying somewhere requires trust, and trust requires a human.

This isn't just a front. Those pilots know how to fly. Several of them are, in fact, my friends from the RAF, and I can attest that some of the best pilots I met in my career are now flying you and your loved ones on commercial airlines. You are in safe hands for two reasons: every pilot is highly trained to begin with, and every pilot continues to hone and refresh those skills to be allowed to keep flying.

The airline industry knows that using the most up-to-date software and operating systems absolutely makes sense to deliver the most efficient and safe service it can. It also knows that we need humans on board who can fly the plane under the most demanding of circumstances. That is a superb example of human–machine partnership. We know what a machine can do well, but we also know we need humans in the loop – and that is why you sometimes have a bumpy landing. Those pilots have to land the plane manually a certain number of times each year, and those bumpy landings are exactly the kind you would be most grateful for if other things went wrong and you were relying solely on your pilot again.

It's not just a theory. In 2009, a flock of geese struck both engines of a passenger plane. Captain 'Sully' Sullenberger successfully pulled off an emergency water landing (or 'ditching') in the Hudson River, which everyone survived.[21] I suspect they were grateful for those bumpy practice landings aviation regulations insist on.

The question of where and how to partner with AI is alive, and it is one you are already wrestling with. Even if you aren't using it at all, you are still making that decision. The example of getting the partnership right between automation and pilot was relatively contained. It was decided within an industry that places a huge premium on safety and regulation.

With AI on your phone and in your workplace, the choice of when and how to use it is initially being made much more organically. Taking the time to think about those choices is imperative for you, both personally and professionally. There are early indications that these choices will matter, for your own skills and for your workplace's ability to maintain and develop them. Good choices now may well insure you against problems later on.

Knowing that we need humans alongside AI is a pretty straightforward principle. Understanding that there are some parts of jobs that should always fall to humans and others that can be better done by machines is uncontroversial. To future-proof yourself and your organisation, you need to go one step further and look at the impact AI is having on us – the human side of that human–AI partnership. There are two clear challenges emerging from the early research: the risk of skills atrophy in your experts, and the risk of there no longer being clear skills pathways for novices to become experts.

Skills atrophy in experts

In 2025, researchers in Poland published findings of a study following nineteen experienced endoscopists. This trial introduced AI assistance into their work to understand the shifts as doctors partnered with AI.[22] The AI system analysed video feeds, highlighting areas where it detected potential abnormalities. The doctors' role shifted from active detection – actively scanning tissue, filtering visual information and recognising patterns – to a different skill: verification.

Three months later, the research team re-measured the doctors' performance, this time without AI assistance. Adenoma detection rates had fallen from 28.4% to 22.4%: a 21% decline. In ninety days, these doctors' foundational skills had already begun to weaken.

This is not a story about technology making us stupid. It is a story about how we learn, how we maintain capability and what happens when the nature of our work fundamentally changes.

The endoscopists had built cognitive fitness in a particular skill: the ability to actively scan, filter and recognise patterns. When AI was introduced, their task shifted from active search to confirmation. The neural pathways associated with that active search began to atrophy – just as muscles weaken when we stop using them – and instead developed for the new requirement.

Let's think about the role of heuristics, which are shortcuts our brain uses to aid the speed of our decisions, often at the expense of accuracy. Dr Gary Klein, who studied expert decision-making in high-pressure fields such as firefighting and military command, identified finely honed heuristics at play. He called it Recognition-Primed Decision (RPD).[23] Experts in these domains don't systematically analyse every option; instead, they recognise patterns based on thousands of previous experiences. A fire commander sees smoke patterns and instantly knows where the fire is spreading. An endoscopist observes tissue texture and knows to look more closely. This pattern recognition requires continuous practice. There's a reason every military serviceperson is asked to practise rifle drills and be tested every year. Remove the foundation of continuous practice, and the ability to recognise more sophisticated tasks will fade.

Why does this matter? We know that we will want humans in the loop for so many areas of professional life, particularly when there is a high level of skill – or human-specific skill – required. The case study of the endoscopists shows just how easily the skills we rely on can erode. An endoscopist supported by AI to be more effective absolutely makes sense, but an endoscopist whose skills shrink so quickly within the first few months of partnering with AI is a warning bell. We are in the foothills of AI adoption; we don't want to lose skills that matter merely for the promise of efficiency.

You will need to make careful choices and plans about how you introduce AI into your workplace. What skills are absolutely essential to your business? What is the human element that you need to interweave with AI? How will you make sure that your team are still practising those skills?

Think about those pilots who fly commercially. Not only are they making sure that they land a plane with enough frequency to keep their licences, but they are also spending a lot of time in simulators to retain those skills. They practise emergencies and unfamiliar landings. What that job looks like has changed – much of the flying is done by technology. The way pilots maintain their skills has changed too; it isn't through flight after flight and landing after landing of manual flying. What hasn't changed? That they have, and they maintain, the high-level skills needed for the job.

You need to think about how you can maintain your critical skills, and you need to clock that the erosion of skills is a swift process – this isn't one that can wait.

Vanishing skills pathways from novices to experts

At the other end of the scale, we have a different problem. As well as worrying about how you keep your experts expert, you will also need to work out how to create them. Every field of endeavour has a tried-and-tested route for building skills. You will know exactly how the professionals in your business currently develop and build their skills – whether it is through a long, established route like medical school or through learning directly on the job.

AI is already disrupting those routes.

I can remember my first few weeks as a management consultant. I was ambitious and eager to prove myself. I can vividly recall the grit, determination and effort that went into my first few months learning the role.

In 2014, day one was research: reading the client's annual reports, studying their industry, attempting to understand what actually mattered to this particular organisation versus what merely seemed important on the surface. Day two was frustrating: constructing an argument, identifying gaps in my thinking, conducting further research and restructuring the logic. The following days and weeks were spent refining, checking assumptions and submitting work to the senior team that I was not entirely confident in.

Crucially, I wasn't just churning my way through results and data. I was learning how to think about client problems. I was building an understanding of how businesses operate, what drives value and how to structure complex information. I was refining my judgement. I was also, through trial and error, learning how to bring my engineering and military experience to this new paradigm – understanding the ways in which I thought through those disciplines and deciding what to bring across and use in my new job. The interactions with senior consultants and partners helped to shape my thinking too. Their feedback helped me spot new patterns in data. They let me know when previous experience was an asset, when it was a hindrance and how to discern the difference. I was building my skills through experience, and through the experience of those around me. I was up to my eyeballs in the discomfort that is critical for development, and I was dependent on thinking with other people.

With the AI resources available to a brand-new management consultant now, those first few days of work look very different indeed. With generative AI, they can input client information and desired outcomes and a draft proposal is generated in minutes. They can refine it, personalise some sections and submit it. The output is often better, more polished, more comprehensive. The consultant is more productive on day one than their predecessors were on day thirty.

With a polished product, however, there is no need for the feedback that I received –the corrections that made me feel uncomfortable as well as the delight I experienced when I got it right. What has our new consultant learnt? How to prompt an AI effectively, and how to edit and refine. They haven't had to sit with the ambiguity of incomplete information and construct an argument anyway. They also haven't experienced the frustration that precedes understanding (we learnt how important that discomfort and frustration are for development in Chapter 2).

Using AI that way is not a stupid choice – it is often the most efficient way to get what looks like the job done – but it cuts out the crucial steps that allow professionals to ascend the skill levels that are required for expertise. You don't need a management consultant to use AI for you, but you might need an experienced management consultant to be a thinking partner in the challenges that threaten your business. The problem is how we grow those management consultants where the early stages of their job – where previously they would be immersed in data and patterns and learning to think about businesses – can be done swifter, and just as well, by generative AI.

This isn't just a management consultant problem. You can repeat this thought experiment with almost any knowledge-based profession. Let's take a completely different example: let's learn from the masters – and I do mean the masters. Leonardo da Vinci apprenticed under Andrea del Verrocchio in Florence for years.[24] He did not begin by painting masterpieces; he sketched water, storms, the proportions of faces and the way fabric drapes. He learnt from his master's approach and dissected corpses to understand the human form from the inside. Most of what he created was never displayed; he was building the capacity to look at a specific situation and know, from deep experience, what approach it required.

Partnering with AI is about ensuring we can still develop the next level of creativity and innovation by knowing what approach is needed. To do that, we can learn from the masters.

The three kinds of knowledge

This is so important that we are going to spend a moment discussing the science of knowledge. Cognitive science distinguishes between three types of knowledge, and they don't develop simultaneously:

1. **Declarative knowledge:** Knowing facts, concepts and definitions. You can acquire this through reading or instruction. You can also, in theory, obtain it from an AI.
2. **Procedural knowledge:** The ability to execute a skill. This requires practice. You don't learn to ride a bicycle by reading about balance; you learn by falling and adjusting.
3. **Conditional knowledge:** The judgement to apply what you know in context. This is the hardest to acquire – and the most valuable. You build it through encountering situations where the answer isn't apparent and you must decide whether it's like previous ones or fundamentally different.

You need the facts first, then you need the procedural knowledge that you learn through practice. Finally, with enough practice, you get to develop that conditional knowledge. You have probably seen this; it looks like a highly experienced operator making a call or even having a gut instinct (I have a story in Chapter 8 that shows what that can look like).

Your entry-level employees need to ascend to that level – that is where your future experts come from. When an AI system can serve up both the facts (the declarative layer) and a good deal on how to implement that knowledge (the procedural layer), you or your employees aren't developing the scaffolding that lets you or them step up to the conditional knowledge – the judgement to apply what they know – because they don't really know it.

Without that, you can't be the partner to AI that a good human–machine partnership should have. You don't face the moment where you must choose or sit with ambiguity. You confirm or reject the system's suggestion. That is a different cognitive task entirely, as the doctors showed us earlier.

In 2014, as a brand-new management consultant, I was building discernment and judgement. In 2026, a brand-new management consultant without additional measures is building dependency.

Create your competitive edge

There is a clear case for careful, deliberate integration of AI into workflows. There is also a clear case for taking the stairs whenever you can (honestly, I still take the lift). We can all look at sage advice, acknowledge that it is absolutely correct and then still do the opposite thing. That's one of the glorious, messy things about being human. It is as clear a vignette as any of why our thinking is more expansive than how we imagine our brain works. If we were the logic machines we imagine we are, receiving well-grounded advice that we should take the stairs or be deliberate with AI integration would result in us, well, taking the stairs and being deliberate with AI.

We are more complicated than that.

In a moment, we'll look at the resistance you might face when trying to be deliberate with AI integration (including from yourself). Before that, I want to pause on the opportunity that this creates for you and for your professional context. The fact that we are complex and not simple logic machines means that there will be real variance in how companies and institutions respond. If you can find a strong enough reason to be deliberate and planful with the AI you use, you will create a competitive edge. Those who refuse AI and those who over-focus on efficiency and removing the human workforce will both miss the real opportunity here.

Those who are considered and deliberate in their use of AI, who take account of challenges like the skills atrophy and stalled development risk, have a real opportunity to create a competitive edge – to be a Netflix rather than a Blockbuster. The competitive edge will be the capability of your humans. Everyone will have access to the AI, but in acquiring it, they may lose the capacity of their humans. Your task is to sustain both.

First, let's look at why the pull to resist solid, well-reasoned advice on AI is so strong.

Resistance

This isn't AI refusal, this is a subtler resistance – the resistance to going thoughtfully and deliberately. With AI already impacted and shaping our personal and professional experience, and its arrival in a world saturated with digital ease, the path of least resistance offers itself as the obvious road.

The path of digital ease is not new, but it is acutely experienced with AI. One of the complicated, lovely paradoxes of being human is that the very things that can build in us strong character and creative skills are the things we will routinely avoid. We know we need discomfort to develop (we've looked at that in detail in the previous two chapters), but we have another drive within us that creates a paradox: humans like the path of least resistance. We like shortcuts. We like saving energy. There's no moral failing in this; we are evolutionary organisms looking for the most efficient way to survive. When these twin truths – the need for discomfort to develop and our default to the path of least resistance – come together in our technology-rich environments, we have a paradox to navigate.

Given the choice, we will avoid choice. It's an odd one, given our great, soaring emphasis on freedom and autonomy as a species. It's why that popular explosion in 'habit hacking' is so prevalent. Habit hacking offers tips on how to make adding a new habit into your routine the path of least resistance, whether that is rolling your yoga mat out before bed, ready for the morning, or putting your vitamins on top of your coffee cup to make sure you take them. We pick the path of least resistance.

AI introduces a risk of meaninglessness. It is not a given that we will meet this existential anxiety by taking the bull by the horns, leaning into what makes us human and leading a creative revolution. We may instead follow our other instinct: outsourcing decisions and judgement to AI, avoiding both choices and the weight of their consequences.

The trap with AI is that by following that path of least resistance we remove the conditions that create competence. We become dependent on the system that is simultaneously making us less capable.

Not only do we need to create a thought-through, deliberate path to the adoption of AI that both preserves human expertise and allows it to develop... we need to do so while working against our instincts that tell us not to do this at all.

It's no wonder that those who master this will create a competitive edge. Let's take a look at how you might begin thinking about this in your work.

Strategies for integrating AI without disintegrating humans

The following idea is designed to generate thinking together as a team on this topic. Chapter 3 spelt out precisely the importance of thinking together. These strategies are far from exhaustive, but I hope they will give you a starting point to generate the conversations in your workplace that help you find that competitive edge.

What has worked for me has been bringing design thinking into the problem space. Back in 2024, I stood in the Helsinki Central Library Oodi in Helsinki, Finland, marvelling at the power that design thinking could bring to problems. They had wanted to build a library to meet the needs of the community. The problem was that there were a number of different needs and they seemed to be mutually exclusive.

Some people wanted a space to quietly study or read – some in silence, some while drinking a coffee.

Others wanted a musical instrument lending library and somewhere to play. Still others wanted the library to be a space that welcomed new parents and young children, to embed the importance of reading from the beginning.

It sounds like an impossible problem to solve, but they used design thinking. Design thinking has the following five principles:

1. **Use human-centred empathy:** Understanding what the community or customer needs – and not just their needs but how they feel and the context of their experience.
2. **Frame the challenge:** Do this in a human-centred way, which is clear and motivated. You will often hear a design-thinking problem begin with the phrase, 'How might we...?'
3. **Generate ideas:** Go for it in coming up with solutions. At this point, don't edit yourself. Include the wild ideas and the seemingly impossible ones.
4. **Prototype and experiment:** Move to finding tangible ways to explore and play with the ideas you are generating. Find out what works and what doesn't.
5. **Bring together different disciplines:** Include people with different specialisms, backgrounds and expertise.

When they applied these principles to the library, an incredible design came into being. The physical layout of the building was designed to mimic sound waves, absorbing the sound of play and music created at one end of the building so that it didn't disturb the quiet study at its heart. You could still grab a book and sit with a coffee to read.

My favourite part was the response to the tension that parents felt in trying to keep their toddlers quiet when their little ones naturally wanted to run and play. Having created a build that could allow sound in one space because it was absorbed without disturbing others, they were able to build an interactive wall, where if you run your hands along it, it plays music and lights up. Not only did it delight the toddlers (and me), it signalled to parents and carers: 'It's OK, they are supposed to make noise here; even the building is making noise.'

What a set of answers for a seemingly intractable problem.

I have brought design thinking to several of my own business challenges and those of my clients. I particularly like the counterintuitive move of centring human needs as we focus on the integration of AI.

It isn't a simple or an easy process but by applying the five-step process and by bringing a human-centred look to questions – such as how you might continue to develop the capacity of your team when the shortcut looks so easy or how you keep your experts match-fit when they aren't required to work at the same skill and intensity as before – you will begin to create real competitive edge. By following a design-thinking approach, you are also exercising exactly what AI cannot do but you can: thinking together with other genuine minds.

FIVE

Kingfisher Moments

'Ava took my job and did it better.' I read the advert as I tapped my phone on the exit barrier on the London Tube. I looked up to see a bigger sign: 'Stop hiring humans'.[25]

I felt affronted. What is it with adverts? First poor old Fatima is out of a ballet career and into a cyber one, and now Ava is coming for my job. 'I don't think so,' I muttered to myself.

Several months later, these adverts by Artisan AI, a Silicon Valley-based startup founded by British entrepreneur Jaspar Carmichael-Jack, immediately came to mind as I began to write this chapter. These were saying the part we fear: What use am *I* then?

I'm going to help with that, and (spoiler) I'm going to tell you the part AI will never be able to do.

Meaning-making

I imagine Jaspar as our modern-day Peter Pan, promising a life of fun and adventure because AI is going to do all the boring work for us, but when we imagine Peter Pan hovering outside the Darling nursery, watching the family reunite, we realise that he has no lasting home, no deep commitment and no real emotional maturity.[26] Ultimately, the cost of permanent childhood is clear: loneliness and stagnation.

Why do we need to grow up, and why must we remember that in an age of AI?

One of the things critical to being a human – in modern life and work – is the ability to make meaning. This might conjure ideas of wellness gurus, ashrams and yoga retreats but it runs deeper. It is important to every aspect of our existence, including the work we do and the workplaces we are part of.

Meaning-making is a psychoanalytic term that comes from the study of human development. Put simply, it is how we make sense of ourselves, our relationships and our place in the world – but it goes further than that. It is not just that sense of creating or deciding a purpose; it is also the integration of all of our senses and our ways of knowing to offer us moments of insight and inspiration.

TE Lawrence wrote, 'Nine-tenths of tactics are certain, and taught in books: but the tenth is like the kingfisher flashing across the pools.'[27] This quote is the reason that the kingfisher is the emblem of the UK Defence Academy's Higher Command and Staff Course, where senior military personnel continue their professional development. It's chosen because this is the point of their careers where senior military commanders have mastered so much through learning and experience, and now must command at an even higher level. At this point, they will need to be open to and create the conditions for the flashes of inspiration through meaning-making that such leadership will demand.

You will have your own moments of that flash of inspiration in your work: a moment when the whole of your experience, integrated and alive, worked at a level that you didn't consciously comprehend, and suddenly a solution appears that was not there a moment before. At a subconscious level, you have been making meaning, which bursts forth in a vivid flash, like a kingfisher darting across the water.

A kingfisher and starling moment in action

One unlikely kingfisher moment that stands out in my memory is when I was a young flight lieutenant on my second deployment to Afghanistan. Being deployed is a heightened experience. It is everything you have studied for, trained for and prepared for. For the months that you are out there, you have worked hard to be in peak condition, knowing that every other aspect of life drops away. There is no life admin. There is no downtime. There is the job, the mission and the team.

On paper, that's exactly what was happening. The things that normally get in the way had been removed. There were no supply issues. We needed parts? We had parts. We had a full complement of people, a fully manned squadron. We were the tip of the spear, with every ounce of the RAF behind us to make sure we could get the job done.

As I worked in the hangar at Bastion, in the searing, dry heat of a Helmand summer, my team were… disheartened. There was a malaise; a loss of confidence had begun to set in. This was particularly worrying as we had recently pulled ourselves out of underperformance and begun to be trusted once again to get the medical evacuation flights out to soldiers in need. I needed to keep my team focused and sharp. Their professional pride, and the lives of others, depended on it.

I wondered what on earth to do about it. I mentally took stock of everything I had been taught in officer training, had learnt in my previous deployments, but nothing was hitting the spot. Which is why I was surprised to find myself ordering my team to gather around while I gave them instructions for an additional task to be taken on and delivered on top of their critical day-to-day mission. It was something to be executed with precision, but not at the expense of our work: to prepare for and execute… the throwing of a party. If I had surprised myself, it wasn't a patch on quite how much I had surprised them.

Nonetheless, their Officer Commanding had just told them that a crucial anniversary was coming up: the Battle of Britain. Although we didn't have the normal resources to mark and celebrate it, I wanted them to create an event to capture what it means to be in the RAF. I told them I needed their creativity and initiative to provide everything we needed, and for it to be acceptable for them to spend time on this, they could not drop a single thing or overlook a single duty. If we were going to get away with throwing a hangar party, they had to be more than good at the day-to-day work; they had to be perfect.

We invited the whole flight line – every crew that flew got an invitation – which meant the Army and Navy too. Service pride was now on the line.

I told them the boundaries and the red lines, and then I trusted them. It felt risky. If a helicopter wasn't ready because they were organising this, the consequences could be unthinkable, but I trusted them.

The appointed day arrived, and I walked into a transformed space. The armourers had made balsa Second

World War aircraft that hung from the ceiling, along with bunting and backdrops. They had built a cocktail bar from wood, with seating and a cinema screen and, in the searing summer heat – miracle of miracles – there was ice. Ice in the upturned damaged bubble-shaped windows from aircraft. When the senior officers arrived, the team had choreographed a ceremony to receive them. The balsa-wood plane turned out to be mobile, as it moved across the hangar and dropped 'bombs' into a reservoir of water, just like the Dambusters. They also honoured a deeply held service tradition, by convincing the Army flight crews – and *only* the Army flight crews – that it was fancy dress.

The hangar rang with laughter, releasing pressure, and for a few precious hours brought together my team and colleagues across the services, uniting us with a past that mattered to our sense of identity. The pride of the unit lay in having done all of this on top of a demanding mission, and in coming up with creative solution after creative solution to bring a moment of novelty and respite to their colleagues.

If you had asked me immediately afterwards why I had done it, I would have said I wanted to give them a task that was high profile but low stakes. Something that would test them to the max as a group, but also something where lives weren't literally – relentlessly – in the balance. Now I have even more sophisticated ways of explaining it. I would say that the group developed its shared ego strength, pushing beyond the boundaries of what it believed it could do.

The honest truth is, in that moment, watching them in the hangar with the seed of an idea germinating, I simply thought it would be good for them. That it might just work. It was a kingfisher moment. A flash of inspiration. It was also a moment where I began to mature, stepping outside of the procedures and the protocol, and started to lead for real. To take risks. To stoke innovation. While we didn't need a balsa-wood spitfire or an ice bucket made from aircraft windows, we absolutely did need the kinds of minds that could conceive original solutions in circumstances where we had next to nothing.

As well as a kingfisher moment, it was a starling moment. One way we can think about our minds is as a murmuration, with our right and left hemispheres in a moving symphony of communication. The left hemisphere potentially holds our capacity for execution – this is where our training, preparation and learning resides. The right hemisphere is our orientation in the world – memory and the integration of experience. It works in symbol… the 'voice' of our mind belongs to the left; the right can only be accessed if we think in the symbols of the insight it offers us, if we can see the kingfisher among the murmuration and act on it.

Developing meaning-making capacity

These kingfisher moments are critical at work. If you are reading this book, it is highly likely that your job demands that you lead through paradox, complexity and uncertainty. That you can make decisions and execute them when your team are feeling mixed emotions: fear and hope, excitement and reluctance. This is what psychoanalysts are describing when they talk about the capacity for meaning-making.

The chances are that you need your team, as well as yourself, to develop that meaning-making capacity. To bring together the right and left hemispheres and create those moments of inspiration. You will know that your team matters the most not just when things are running on rails, but when things go wrong – when the context changes, when the competition is hot, when things break or get hard. That's when you need a team that can innovate, imagine and find inspiration. One that can dig in and find the grit to navigate a way through. The team that you need is one that has the capacity for meaning-making.

How is that capacity built? From the last chapter, you know that there are no shortcuts. People need to ascend the maturity scales through development, experience and learning to act on their own kingfisher moments. Without that, they remain the Peter Pan figure at the beginning of the chapter, locked outside the house of development through a refusal to take the uncomfortable steps of growing up.

This capacity of meaning-making is critical to work, but research is beginning to imply that this capacity is also vulnerable to disruption by AI. It is one of those critical capacities that can't be replaced by AI, either.

Why can't AI make meaning?

You may wonder if it is just a matter of time before AI develops a meaning-making function. I imagine the former Chief AI Scientist of Meta, Yann LeCun, would agree. In an interview published in 2026, he stated that LLMs will never have superintelligence as they are constrained by language and the need to understand how the world works.[28] The architecture that he is working on now will interpret world views and rely on 'emotions', meaning past experiences and evaluations will also guide its predictions.

This does not provide a meaning-making function in a psychoanalytic sense, and here's why.

The hemispheres of our brain are not modular components but deeply integrated aspects of a unified organism that breathes and physically feels. We may be able to watch our hemispheres light up on a brain scan, but they are activated because our bodies are sending them a miracle and a multitude of signals from our physical, embodied world, connecting us on so many levels to our environment. To survive, we must come up against friction in everyday life, we must experience mutual vulnerability that we have in human communication. We are brilliantly unpredictable and we forget – we have to or we become overwhelmed. We also live in time; AI will not miss you if you don't log in for a couple of weeks.

AI models currently aim to mimic some of the neural networks in our brains, but not our bodies:

- **Symbolic AI:** This is akin to the left hemisphere of the brain. It uses explicit symbols and rules that machines manipulate to solve complex problems.
- **Statistical AI:** This is closer to the right hemisphere of the brain. Machines learn directly from data rather than pre-programmed rules.
- **Neurosymbolic AI:** This merges the two, combining the learning capabilities of statistical AI with the interpretability and logical structure of symbolic approaches, offering an (albeit reductive) analogy for how we make decisions.

This is a rudimentary cartoon of how we work, failing to take account of our embodied existence in a physical environment. It doesn't truly capture our embodied signals or even our emotions.

Emotion and the left and right hemispheres

Think of the word emotion: *e-motion*. It developed from the French for 'to stir up', tapping into an idea that emotions are internal stirrings. Children learn words from the way it makes them feel in their bodies.

Jaak Panksepp, who defined the term 'affective neuroscience',[29] created an equation to show just how complex the information the brain receives from the body: 'The affect (memory of the 7 primary emotions (seeking, care, play, lust, anger, fear, sadness)) + Visceral sensation (sight, sound, taste, temperature etc) + Hormones = feedback to the brain.' This feedback is then engaged by the two hemispheres: right and left.

The right hemisphere's engagement with the world involves qualities that remain deeply mysterious: phenomenal consciousness, genuine understanding and the apprehension of meaning and value. Yet this hemisphere is more prone to self-doubt and uncertainty and, crucially, lacks direct access to the motor speech centre; it has no voice. It is our unconscious.

The left hemisphere excels at focused analysis, explicit reasoning and the systematic unpacking of implicit knowledge into manipulable components. It provides the precision, categorisation and sequential processing necessary for detailed work. This hemisphere's certainty comes at the cost of contextual awareness; it cannot see the Gestalt – the ultimately indivisible whole – and therefore believes it can operate independently when it cannot. It is our ego.

For meaning-making to occur, the feedback our brain receives must move from right hemisphere to left hemisphere and back again. The contribution of the left hemisphere is valuable but must come at an intermediate stage. Problems with developing meaning-making capability arise when this analytical phase is treated as the endpoint rather than a step in an ongoing cycle.

Meaning-making is not just about understanding why something happened. It's about integrating one's expertise, intuition, gut feeling, judgement and life experience to deepen one's understanding of the Gestalt: the impact of the self, the team, the organisation. This is a continual, circular process.

Why is the development of capacity vulnerable to AI?

This is where early research becomes interesting – and, if we are wise, alarming. A series of studies from 2025, involving 3,500 participants, found that the removal of AI from workers who had been using it had a big impact on their intrinsic motivation and tolerance for boredom.[30] Groups were given typical office tasks: writing emails, brainstorming and drafting Facebook posts. Some had access to generative AI, while others didn't. The groups with access performed well, producing polished writing that conveyed warmth and connection. When the support of generative AI was removed and they had to complete a task without it, their motivation dropped and their boredom levels increased.

If you want to be able to have moments of inspiration – and if you want your team to be creative and innovative – they need that intrinsic motivation and the ability to sit with tasks without giving into boredom (in Chapter 2 we established how critical discomfort is to our development). This is another example of the same principle: to reach meaning-making and inspiration, we need the stamina to stay with the discomfort of boredom.

Without that, we risk becoming lost. It's no accident that the children who chose to stay with Peter Pan – to flee boredom and routine – were named the Lost Boys. The paradox is that it is staying with the trouble, working the boundary between the everyday and learning the work inside out, that builds in us the capacity to rise to an occasion, to think new thoughts and to generate novel solutions. Without that, we cannot mature. We never grow up. We don't make meaning.

With AI in the workplace, you have a tremendous tool for efficiency and productivity, but without deliberate curation and choice in how it is used, it can arrest the development of both you and your team. Human–machine partnering relies on us being able to do the things that the machines cannot – or should not – do. Meaning-making is something that machines cannot do, and humans must. Creating an integration of AI that preserves this critical human capacity is not just a wise move, it's a commercially competitive one.

People's ability to develop expertise, intuition, gut feeling, judgement and life experience comes from human–human interaction, which allows us to learn from experience. Developmental psychology – using research that goes back decades – shows us that human meaning-making capacity evolves through stages. People move from conventional thinking (based on rules and social norms) towards post-conventional thinking (based on principles and the integration of competing values and perspectives).[31] These are not stages we are born into; these are stages we develop through encountering situations that our current way of understanding cannot handle, sitting with the discomfort that creates and gradually builds new mental structures capable of greater complexity. The further along them we develop, the greater our capacity for meaning-making becomes.

You may have come across the 'levels of thinking' in leadership books and psychometric tests. The Holy Grail of leadership theory is to be able to ascend to post-conventional thinking, the ability to tolerate ambiguity and reframe, challenge and even rewrite rules. A hallmark of post-conventional thinking is the capacity to hold conflicting truths simultaneously. The mature mind does not split the world into binaries of 'good/bad' or 'right/wrong'. The post-conventional mind can hold the tension of opposites (such as being both strong and vulnerable, rational and intuitive) without collapsing them. This capacity to sit with paradox is what allows for 'transformational' rather than merely 'transactional' leadership. It is crucial for meaning-making.

Organisations that lack people with mature meaning-making capacity may process information efficiently, but they are only effective when conditions are well-structured and systems are working. They become brittle when facing novel problems or system failure.

How do you develop meaning-making for yourself and your team?

Practice, of course. We could take a leaf out of the White Queen's book from *Through the Looking Glass*,[32] and try to believe at least six impossible things before breakfast, or we can follow the idea of Carl Jung and develop our 'symbolic attitude'.[33] This is the term he uses to describe the ability to hold onto something not yet fully formed and to sit with the discomfort of not knowing. (Again, we are back to Chapter 2 and the importance of discomfort.) Even the Romantic poets cared about this one, with Keats calling it 'negative capability'.[34] In this attitude, you recognise that patience, uncertainty and tolerance are not passive states where difficulty washes over you, but active capacities that allow ideas and solutions to emerge. Remember the idea about how our right and left brains operate? If you can remain in that state of not knowing, you are giving the creative space for your right hemisphere to offer ideas through symbols and images.

Iceberg journalling

I recognise that strolling into your Monday morning team meeting and declaring that you want to pursue symbolic attitude while quoting Lewis Carroll and Keats might not be the most effective way to bring your team around. Instead, ask yourself: As a leader, how do I develop meaning-making capacity in my team?

It begins with you, before you bring this to your team. At its heart, developing those higher-level capacities is all about paying deliberate attention to both the situations and relationships you are in, and noticing how you respond. To help with this, I want to share a deliberate, written self-reflection exercise: iceberg journalling.

Think of your challenge, relationship situation or question like an iceberg. It has a small part sitting above the water but the bulk of it lies beneath, at the unconscious layer. By paying deliberate attention, you can make some of the unconscious conscious. The act of reflecting also develops patience – the ability to sit with the half-known – and creates space for the right and left hemispheres to interact.

To begin, write down the tip of the iceberg: the part that you can clearly see. What happened? What words were used? What was the situation? Try to make it as accurate a reflection as you can.

Next, dive below the waterline to explore what is happening one layer down. Start by writing down your physical response – How did your body react to the situation? – then see if you can recall your thoughts in the moment. After that, write down the story you are telling yourself about the situation. Finally, re-read what you have written and think about the meaning you want to deliberately create from this situation. How will you choose to move forward?

Here is an example to help you.

An example of iceberg journalling

Question	Example
The tip of the iceberg: what happened?	My boss told me that the report I submitted wasn't good enough to be the final draft, and that I needed to meet with her to discuss how to improve it before it could be finalised. She spoke to me as we were both leaving the weekly team meeting, then hurried off to her next meeting.
What do I recall about my physical response?	As she spoke to me, I felt my stomach drop away and a burning sensation at the back of my eyes. I could feel the adrenaline spike in the tension across my neck and shoulders. After she walked away, I felt a bit wobbly and zoned out from everyone else who was chatting around me.

(Continued)

Question	Example
What thoughts were in my mind?	I thought I had done a good job, I felt disappointed and a bit embarrassed. What had I missed?
What story was I telling myself?	'The report wasn't good enough,' but I was telling myself that *I* wasn't good enough.
Does this remind me of anything?	It reminds me of my university dissertation feedback, when my whole future career felt like it depended on my degree result.
What meaning shall I make?	This is where you have agency. Ask yourself: What do I now understand about myself? How might this be a strength? How might this show up as a stumbling block? What have I learnt?

These prompts are just to get you started. The most important thing is to build a habit of reflecting, ideally through writing, to help you notice and develop your meaning-making capacity. This is one of the things that AI really can't do, and by developing it in yourself, you create a competitive edge.

Deepening your listening

Once you have done that, see if you can go one step deeper. This is something I learnt in my psychoanalytic training. The Jungian discipline I trained in places great emphasis on the symbolic language of the unconscious as a way of giving us clues about how we actually are feeling.

You can do this in your own self-reflection and when discussing things as a team. Notice how you – or a team member – describe what's happening, paying real attention to the tone and the language being used.

Here are some prompt questions to help you tune in to that extra level of listening:

- What is your / their role in the story? Are you / they a helper, a villain, an onlooker or something else?
- Is the telling a summary or is it full of detail?
- What seems most important: facts, feelings, sense impressions or embodied response?
- Where is your agency in the story? Did it happen to you or did you drive it?
- What kind of language is being used? Is it literal or are there metaphors? What kind?

This is a way to deepen your listening and your meaning-making capacity even further. There isn't a 'right' answer to any of this, the aim isn't to diagnose the problem perfectly or find a neat solution. It is to increase your ability to sit with the questions and uncertainty and, while tolerating that discomfort, to dig deeper into it rather than flinching away. That act alone develops your meaning-making capacity.

The power of drawing

Another helpful exercise is to stay with pens and paper and draw. You don't have to be a great artist to benefit from this, but you do have to be strict and stick to pictures rather than words. This is a great way to engage the right hemisphere directly, as it works in symbols. Set yourself the challenge of drawing your situation, the relationships in your team, or what it might look like when a problem has been resolved. Scribble away, use colour and don't judge yourself on artistic merit. You aren't competing for the Turner prize; you are offering your right hemisphere a direct outlet for its symbolic thinking. Get it down on the page and see if your thinking shifts – you might be surprised by its power.

Collective identity through storytelling

We have been focusing largely on you as a leader, helping you to find ways to develop your meaning-making capacity. Here's a step you can take with your team.

It begins with storytelling. Storytelling is our collective way of making sense of the world. Our ancestors wrote myths and stories to be told in times of paradox, struggle and inner conflict, helping us make meaning of difficult situations to see that a way through is possible. (I can't be the only one who has muttered, 'Once more unto the breach, dear friends!' when asking a team to do one more push to get something over the line.) We can seek comfort in understanding that people have been battling with the situations we face today for millennia. We may have different ways of telling the stories now but they still aid the connection that we are not alone.

The stories that emerge in these moments help us connect with those who shared the experience and reframe events so that we can learn from them and recall them in meaningful ways. Research on how storytelling and memory work together is both fascinating and underlines this point in bold: we don't lay down memories properly until we have found a way to turn them into a story.

This means that making space for storytelling – and recalling events and situations together – is a powerful technique, not just for building a sense of team identity but also for developing meaning-making capacity across your wider team. You already may run retrospectives to explore what went well and what didn't on challenges and projects. Try using that deeper exploration we looked at for your own self-reflection, and pay attention to how people are talking about their experience in your team.

Have a think about what stories you want to tell and internalise as a team. Talking about work together is a meaning-making exercise. In whichever way you approach it, you are – in a way – telling stories together, and when you tell stories together you create meaning together – you begin to think together.

Make sure you linger in this space longer than you currently do. It can feel indulgent to reflect on things as a team – even like time wasted – but this is deeply important work. It develops your team's capacity to do the work that only humans can do. There is an important tradition in the military of 'spinning dits' – that is, telling stories – which we will explore later in Chapter 7. I can promise you, if the military not only allows for this but deliberately makes time for it, it tells you that this is a valuable practice.

It doesn't just have to happen at the end of something; storytelling is a practice you can begin a project with. Look back to the design-thinking process we explored in Chapter 4. Asking the question 'How might we...' is a wonderful way in which we can begin building a story together.

The goal here is to make sure that you can develop and do the things that AI can't. Not because you are competing with it, but because you are partnering with it. In great partnerships, you want to be able to lean into the unique things each can bring.

You can also try the drawing exercise (discussed earlier in the chapter) with your team, even as part of the storytelling exercise. Get out those pens and paper and invite them to draw the story, or the problem, or what might help. Ban words from the pages and help them connect with their right hemispheres.

If you are feeling adventurous, you can ask them to describe the picture to you before showing it, while you – or another member of your team – draw it yourselves. Compare the two drawings when they are finished. What didn't they describe? What's missing between the pictures? Where does it look the same? Where is it different?

Now you are thinking together, just as we explored in Chapter 3. Even more powerfully, you are thinking symbolically together – and making meaning.

SIX

Building Spaces And Connections

When I was thirteen, I had – unlikely as it sounds – a life-changing conversation with a careers adviser. At that point, my world was sport. I played on the school hockey, lacrosse and tennis teams. I represented the school in athletics, competing in javelin and high jump. When she asked me what I wanted to do for a career, I said simply, 'Something where I can play sport and where every day is different.' Rather than laughing at my idea of what a job might be, she didn't miss a beat and suggested the Army, pointing me towards the cadets as a way to see if I might enjoy it.

A week later, I found myself hesitating on the edge of an Army barracks, in the gloom of a Tuesday evening in January in Edinburgh, daunted at the thought of stepping across the threshold into this unknown space.

My first surprise was that I had inadvertently turned up at the air cadets, rather than the Army cadets (who met the following day, on Wednesdays). Having got myself there and through the door, I wasn't about to back away over so small a distinction as to which of the services I would ultimately join. A magnetic quality to the atmosphere drew me in. There was a hum of purpose to this group of teenagers, a palpable discipline and focus in the room. I went back the following week, the week after and the week after that. In the end, I served a decade in the Air Force.

If you had asked me at the time why I carried on after that first session, I might have listed the opportunities: international travel, learning to fly before I could drive, playing sport across the UK. In truth, it wasn't that. It was the hum and the focus of that room and the promise of something worthwhile.

It was decades later that I was able to recognise what the instructors had built there; a strong container where friendships could flourish and teenagers could find within themselves qualities and talents they didn't yet know they possessed. It was also a space that we ourselves, as cadets, built up, forming links between us that, in some cases, lasted a lifetime.

AI navigating transformation

Navigating the road to adulthood is one of the biggest transformations we undergo as humans, so when we turn to business-based change challenges, it shouldn't surprise us that the architecture of what works well with teenagers also underpins other significant transformation, in both business and life.

When that change is AI, we are learning that there is a new complicating factor. It is no longer just, 'How do I navigate this latest change?' but also, 'What is AI doing to the tools and methods I use to navigate change?' The methods used by the air cadets are no exception. They created a container and fostered linking.

To create a container is to build a psychological and structural space within a group that allows them to complete a task without becoming derailed. It sets out a beginning, a middle and an end to the task, and creates a space that can withstand the emotion and change required to complete it. One of the elements that is always necessary is linking. Linking describes the connections that occur between people in the group – how they share ideas and thoughts together to make meaning.

Differences in organisational approaches to adopting AI

Let's imagine two organisations are setting out to adopt AI. First, we will see how containers and linking either support or block the success of the change. Second, we'll think about how AI itself is impacting those techniques.

In the first organisation, the adoption is announced through clear metrics: the percentage of employees using the tool, time saved per task, productivity gains by department and overall AI usage.

In the second organisation, the adoption is announced with a different framing. There is structured space to experiment, explicit permission to raise concerns about workflow changes and protection for time spent learning to use tools thoughtfully. There is an acknowledgement that premature optimisation carries risk, and that some jobs require more learning by doing than others. Performance is not measured by speed of adoption but by the preservation of capability.

Both organisations are adopting the same tool. The organisational environment around the adoption, however, is very different. What happens next?

The first is mechanistic. It doesn't understand how group structures work or what people need from them to function well. The second does understand this, and it puts in place for its employees the kind of experience that I had through air cadets as a teenager. That company absolutely asks its employees to step outside of their comfort zone – to experiment and learn new things. It does so within a supportive structure: one that works alongside its employees as they take that journey, treats them as adults with agency and ideas and listens to their concerns. They have built the container.

Work group functioning and basic assumption mentality

We talked in Chapter 3 about the importance of creating a space where we can think together. My air cadet instructors provide a clear example of how to do that. More specifically, Bion distinguished between work group functioning – where people are genuinely engaged with the actual task, willing to face difficulty, capable of challenging each other's assumptions and learning together – and basic assumption functioning, where defensive, anxiety-driven patterns take over and people operate from a place of threat rather than genuine engagement.[35] The air cadets gave me the former, teaching me to face challenges and difficulty with grit and determination, supported by peers who both depended on me and cheered me on. (The Marines are exceptionally good at this, but more on them in Chapter 8.)

In a 'work group mentality' (the one the air cadets did so well), members focus on the task itself. They assess effectiveness. They think critically about whether what they are doing serves the purpose. Think back to the best teams you have had the fortune to work with – whether in your professional life, a sports team or an art project. You have probably experienced the kind of flow I am talking about. There is a clear sense of purpose and a strong commitment from everyone in that group to get the job done. Whether staging a play, competing in a tournament or delivering a project, everyone is there to deliver the goal.

When anxiety rises – when the task feels too difficult or uncertainty becomes too uncomfortable – groups shift into what Bion called 'basic assumption mentality'.[36] The group's behaviour becomes driven not by reality but by unconscious emotional states designed to avoid facing it. Have you ever experienced that? When a group begins to fracture and, instead of holding each other, you can feel it disintegrating around you.

Weirdly, any emotion can destabilise a group and risk it moving from that productive state to this one. It's not just anxiety or fear; it can be excitement. I once worked for a company that was on the verge of being bought out. For a lot of the employees who were shareholders, there was the promise of a significant payout, so there was a lot of anticipation and excitement. Because people couldn't speak freely about what that might mean – perhaps retiring early or leaving to follow a passion-project – the atmosphere changed and we flipped into basic assumption mentality. That meant a rocky start after the buyout and some difficult cultural changes that took a long time to work through.

Bion (who came up with these ideas) identified three basic assumptions that groups unconsciously adopt when they flip into avoiding their actual work: dependency, fight–flight and pairing. I think of these as traps, and in organisations adopting AI, I have seen all three spring.

Trap 1: Dependency – waiting for the system to save us

In the dependency trap, the group behaves as if its purpose is to be sustained by a leader or a system that will provide for all needs and solve all problems. The group waits passively for rescue. When AI adoption triggers this pattern, organisations act as if the technology itself will solve their problems, without requiring genuine change in how people work or think.

Think about an organisation that introduces AI tools with promises of transformation. Leaders speak about AI as if it will automatically improve decision-making, accelerate work and solve longstanding productivity challenges. The message – explicit or implicit – is: adopt the system and your problems will be resolved.

Staff respond by waiting. They attend training and access the tools, but they do not actively engage with the more complex questions:

- What does this change about how I need to think?
- What capability do I need to develop alongside this tool?
- When should I use it and when should I rely on my own judgement?

Instead, there is a passive hope that the system, or the leaders who introduced it, will magically make everything work.

The dependency pattern creates employees who outsource their own capacity for thinking and decision-making onto a leader – and get stuck. In AI adoption, this projection shifts from leaders to the technology itself. Workers project their thinking capacity onto the AI then wait for it to solve problems they would previously have worked through themselves.

When the AI inevitably fails to deliver magical solutions, produces errors, requires significant human judgement to use well and creates new problems, the group does not adapt. Instead, it replaces one dependency with another. It waits for the next version of the tool, for better training and for leaders to fix the implementation. It does not take responsibility for its own development.

Trap 2: Fight–flight – finding enemies in adoption

In the fight–flight trap, the group behaves as if there is an enemy that must either be attacked or fled from. The group oscillates between these two responses but commits decisively to neither. When AI adoption triggers this pattern, the 'enemy' can take many forms: the technology itself, other teams adopting faster, workers who resist adoption or leaders pushing implementation.

Imagine a team introducing AI writing tools. Some team members immediately resist: 'This will destroy our writing quality. This is lazy. We're losing essential skills.' They fight the adoption. Others withdraw: they attend the training but never actually use the tools, they cite workload or technical difficulties, or they quietly maintain old workflows. They flee from engagement.

The team meeting becomes a site of oscillation. One week, the fight dominates: heated debate about whether AI threatens professional standards, whether it should be restricted and whether specific uses should be banned. The following week, flight dominates: the conversation shifts entirely away from AI, focusing instead on unrelated administrative matters and avoiding the uncomfortable reality that the organisation has mandated adoption but the team has not resolved how to respond.

What is avoided in both fight and flight is the actual work: genuinely engaging with what AI means for the team's capability, developing thoughtful integration strategies, acknowledging both benefits and risks, and making concrete decisions about where and how to use these tools. A group can be in danger of spending the whole of its weekly team meeting on a matter without resolving it, because resolution would require facing the anxiety that the fight–flight pattern is designed to avoid.

The fight–flight pattern also manifests between teams. One department adopts AI aggressively and begins criticising others for moving too slowly. Another resists and frames adoption as reckless or unprofessional. Both are fighting, but neither is genuinely assessing what adoption means for capability development. The organisation becomes fragmented, with some groups rushing forward, others retreating and no one engaging in the actual work of thoughtful integration.

Trap 3: Pairing – hoping the right combination will save us

In the pairing trap, the group behaves as if salvation will come from a future event or an unborn solution produced by a pairing between two parties. The group focuses entirely on the future as a defence against the difficulties of the present. There is hopeful anticipation that the right combination of people, systems and ideas will solve everything, but this hope is never tested against reality.

In AI adoption, this trap appears as magical thinking about what will happen when certain conditions are met. 'Once we have better AI tools, everything will improve.' 'When AI and human expertise properly integrate, we'll achieve breakthrough productivity.' 'If leadership and technical teams align on strategy, adoption will succeed.' The language is always future-oriented, always conditional and always vague about what needs to happen now.

Imagine a strategic planning meeting where an organisation is discussing AI implementation. Much time is spent on aspirational statements about the future state: how work will transform, how capability will expand, how competitive advantage will emerge. There is excitement in the room and people feel energised by the vision. When the meeting ends, little has been decided about concrete next steps. No one has committed to specific changes in how they work. No one has acknowledged the difficulty of the transition or the capability development it requires.

The pairing trap keeps hope alive while avoiding action.

In organisations, the pairing trap often manifests as waiting for two groups to come together to solve the problem. 'When IT and operations properly collaborate on AI implementation…', 'When senior leadership and frontline managers align…', 'When the AI vendor and our internal team coordinate…'. The focus is always on the hoped-for alignment rather than on what each party needs to do independently.

Do you recognise any of these three issues for your business or institution? If you do, you need to think not just about the container but also about 'linking' – what happens when groups can think together or what doesn't happen when they can't.

From traps to linking

Earlier, I described linking as the way that groups shared thoughts and ideas to create meaning. Bion developed this concept to describe the psychological and emotional connections that hold groups together.[37] Links involve both how we feel and how we think. They form when one person genuinely understands another – when emotional resonance occurs alongside intellectual exchange.

These links can be attacked, disrupted, severed or prevented from forming, leaving people isolated from each other, even when they are in the same room. Just as when a mother is too anxious, defensive or absent, the infant's experience is not contained. The infant learns that emotional connection is dangerous, that projecting feelings into another brings retaliation or abandonment rather than relief, and begins to attack the very mechanism – linking – through which development happens.

What happens in infancy establishes patterns that persist into adult organisational life. When workers encounter an organisational environment that cannot tolerate genuine concern, that deflects or punishes emotional honesty or that responds to projected anxiety with defensiveness rather than containment, the early pattern repeats. People learn again that linking is dangerous. They withdraw into isolation, protect themselves through disconnection, and the capacity for genuine thinking together collapses.

Attacks on linking

Take a moment and think about the challenges you and your team are navigating. I don't know the specifics, but given the world we are in I can make a prediction that they are complex, they involve uncertainty, they require a careful dance between technology and creativity, and they come with immediate answers. What do you need most from your team in those moments? The opposite of what I have described above. You need a team to be rich in the links between them: to be connected, to think creatively together and to hold that container in that almost magical space where they are focused and working as a unit.

An organisation structured only around speed, metrics and rapid productivity gains tends to trigger those three traps – and the attacks on linking that follow. When AI adoption is framed as competitive (first-movers win), threat-driven (adopt or fall behind) or mandate-based (this is how we now work), the psychological environment shifts. People move into fight-or-flight mode: competitive adoption races, ranking by AI tool usage, pressure to demonstrate fluency. The space for genuine human connection – for people to think together, to acknowledge uncertainty and to recognise concern – collapses. The links are attacked.

This happens in subtle ways. Think about a meeting where an AI adoption initiative is being rolled out. Someone worries, 'What if we lose independent capability in this area? Should we slow down?' In an organisation operating where the traps are activated, these questions can't be genuinely heard and considered.

1. **In the dependency trap**, the concern is deflected; someone declares: 'Leadership has made this decision; we need to trust the process.'
2. **In the fight–flight trap**, the concern is treated as an attack: 'Why are you resisting this? Other teams are moving much faster.'
3. **In the pairing trap**, the concern is deferred: 'We'll address that once we've fully implemented the system and seen how it works.'

In all three cases, the person who raised the concern experiences a rebuff. They are not heard. Their concern is not genuinely considered. The linking is attacked, the potential connection between that person and others – around the genuine complexity of the question they raised – is interrupted and deflected.

This process can become self-reinforcing. Once attacks on linking begin, they spread. People who are not genuinely heard become less available for genuine contact with others. This reinforces others' decisions to withdraw. What emerges is an organisational environment where communication still happens but emotional linking is excluded – where people speak from their own preoccupations without genuinely connecting to the concerns of others.

Imagine a team being encouraged to adopt an AI writing assistant. The first three people who express concern that the tool might atrophy writing skills are each told, separately, some variation of: 'This is what we're doing; you need to get comfortable with it,' or 'Other teams are moving much faster than you.' Each person experiences this as a deflection. Their actual concern is not addressed. They are treated as problems to be managed rather than people with legitimate questions.

After this happens three times, what happens in the fourth team meeting, when a new person is thinking about raising a concern? They see the pattern. They stay quiet. The linking is attacked. The possibility of the team thinking together about the real implications of this change disappears.

Here is the kicker when the change being introduced is AI: there is somewhere also to go when people stay quiet. There is an alternative place to take concerns, worries and questions – to the AI itself. In one way, you might celebrate that people are turning to the AI, even if it is for an easier way to handle their questions and discomfort.

It matters how the teams engage with AI. If they turn to it because it is somewhere they can explore their worries without risking being shut down in a meeting – somewhere to soothe their concerns and relieve their discomfort – then you have a problem. You have a connection with AI that is compounding isolation and disconnection and creating exactly the attacks on linking that undermine a good container. This time it's happening with the help of the very tool you were hoping to integrate to create a better team.

It's tricky, right?

Defining a shared purpose

We know how to do this. It takes courage, it takes patience and it takes a willingness to sit with discomfort. If you crack those things, two crucial outcomes follow:

1. You can deliver complex change
2. You can bring the human portion of the human–AI partnership.

Here's how we do it.

We define a purpose. Remember 'work group mentality'? When everyone shared that purpose and the container was healthy? It depended on a shared purpose. A simple way to diagnose that is a 'silent disco brainstorm'. Gather your team or your senior leadership team, and ask them to write down on a sticky note – without conferring – the purpose of a team. Once they're done, ask them to stick the notes on the wall. Do they match? If you don't have a matching set, that's your first task. Start there and work out what your shared purpose is.

Building the container by addressing assumptions

Purpose alone isn't enough; we also need to build the container. Even where a shared purpose exists there is plenty of scope for the container to go wrong, so stick with the silent disco brainstorm exercise, but this time ask everyone to write down their top five assumptions. This might be things like:

1. 'I assume I can work from home.'
2. 'I assume you will provide IT.'
3. 'I assume we are all available Monday to Friday.'
4. 'I assume marketing supports me.'
5. 'I assume that I am responsible for product development.'

As the leader, you have to address those assumptions. Not all of them will stand, and you will have some of your own. This is where the human work kicks in. As you start this conversation, know that you are going to need to deliver messages that may be uncomfortable (maybe they can't work from home or rely on marketing), and you might also need to receive challenge and new ideas. This is the space where you can model – and enable – genuine connection.

Defining principles – the inversion test

Next, with purpose agreed and assumptions addressed, it is time to talk principles. How will this group run? You will doubtless have sat in a lot of workshops over your career where principles are agreed. I suspect several of them will have had a real 'motherhood and apple-pie' feel. Perhaps you set out values such as integrity and teamwork. These aren't the principles I want you to forge. The principles you create here have to pass the inversion test.

This is simple. If you said the opposite, would it still be something you were willing to do? For example, putting down 'we work with integrity' doesn't pass the test. No one worth working with would sign up to the principle that 'we do not work with integrity'. It's a no-brainer. It's probably a moral rule. Those aren't the principles we are looking for.

The principles we want are the ones that really say something about this group and this purpose – and that would still make sense if you inverted them. One example is diversification versus making a bet. You might choose to spread your chances, making sure the team has a finger in several pies, or you might want to go all-in on a big bet and focus the team on making that work – both are sound strategies, depending on the circumstances. By choosing one, you are setting a principle.

Another example would be the centralisation of enabling functions versus local control. One lets you centre efficiency; the other gives greater control at a local level. Both have their place under the right circumstances and either is a genuine choice. Once you choose between them, you have defined a principle.

Creating a container

Consider the genuine choices you have to navigate as a team. Where are their tensions, disputes and questions to resolve? This will point you to where your principles need to be forged. Do that work together and you begin to create a container.

This is just the beginning. The container you build – the one underpinned by purpose and principles – is not static. If you want the team to keep flourishing, you need to make sure that the container keeps evolving with you. Keep leaning into the difficult conversations, testing those assumptions and checking whether those principles are still serving you and your team or whether they need to be updated.

Team written exercise for moving from traps to linking

Steps to address the traps (Get the team to do this in silence on sticky notes)	From traps to linking
What's the purpose of the team?	Do they match? If you don't have a matching set, that's your first task. Start there and work out your shared purpose.
What are your top five assumptions?	Start to build the container. As the leader, you have to address those assumptions. Not all of them will stand – and you will have some of your own.
What are your principles?	The principles you are going to create have to pass the inversion test (could the opposite be true)? If yes, it's a principle; if no, it's a rule.

PART THREE

BEING A BODY AND HAVING A MIND

SEVEN
Trust

There is a paradox in AI research with which scientists have been wrestling for decades. If you have ever laughed at a clumsy robot struggling with seemingly simple human tasks, you have seen the paradox in action yourself. It is called Moravec's paradox,[38] and the crux of it is that evolution spent millions of years honing our sensorimotor skills and only recently added a thin veneer of abstract reasoning. Chess, maths and complex logic are all things with which we grapple and struggle, while a young child can hop, skip and jump their way through an afternoon of play, their bodies performing extraordinary feats while their minds take flights of fancy. For AI, the reverse is true. It can whizz through complex computation in moments but even the simplest of animal motions and embodied tasks trouble it.

One of the most critical competencies for us, as we begin to integrate AI into our professional and personal lives, is to think clearly about what it is and what it isn't. That's crucial for making good decisions about where we do use AI, and where we shouldn't. It sounds a simple thing to do; AI is great for synthesising large amounts of data, but it is probably not best placed to replace my therapist.

Because of how we have learnt to think about ourselves, we've made the task of thinking well about AI quite a lot harder.

Embracing embodiment

Moravec's paradox points us to an absolutely critical difference between humans, human intelligence and AI. Humans are deeply embodied creatures in and of the world. There has been a recent explosion of understanding that our own intelligence isn't a brain in a jar operating a meat suit that moves through the world. We know that we 'think' in our hearts and our guts, that our endocrine system does a beautiful ballet with our hormones, that cortisol, adrenaline and oxytocin all impact how we think.

We have a strong tradition, particularly in the Western world, of identifying the human part of us as purely the mind. I must say, I blame Descartes for this. In his brilliantly bonkers thought experiment – How do I know an evil demon isn't deceiving me about everything? – he coined the term 'I think, therefore I am.'[39] He leant into our rationality, our mind, as our uniquely human functioning, taking down deceptive evil demons and laying the matter to rest. This phrase severs our mind from our body and deifies it. It enshrines reason as the best bit of us and dismisses the body as base. That single thought has underpinned much of how we think and reason about ourselves and the world.

If we want to think well about AI, we need to ditch the Descartes and embrace embodiment as central to our human-ness. If we do that, we can begin to think well about the place of AI in our businesses, institutions and lives. At the moment, there is still a lot of muddied thinking, and because we have come to associate the mind as the most human part of us, we risk thinking of AI as human too. It's not. It can be a welcome part of our world, but it can't be human – however much it may speak like us and mimic our neural networking.

Art is a wonderful example. We instinctively know that there is something false about AI-generated art. We feel tricked if we find out a song or a poem was created by AI. Why? Art is a connection between creatures. I feel a certain sensation and want to capture it. I write about love, or missing someone, or how the smell of lilacs can take me back to the summer I first fell in love. You read that, and remember your own scents, sensations and feelings. If AI had generated a poem, you have words that mimic poetry or song, but they come from something that has never felt the ache of missing someone or smelt the perfume of lilacs drifting up to an open window on a warm summer's night.

This embodiment is our human advantage. In the following chapters, I talk about three areas in which embodiment is critical for leaders. The embodied leader, in a world with AI, is the leader with an advantage: the leader who can do things that AI never can, while using AI to sharpen their business, operations or delivery. In business, there is a saying that you have to be the best or you have to be unique. The things that might have set you apart as a brilliant leader in the decades before AI – whip-smart thinking, attention to detail and numerical literacy – will become universal advantages for anyone competent in using AI to support them. A universal advantage is no advantage at all.

Leaning into what AI can never be does let you create an advantage. If you can lead with embodied presence, if you can develop expertise in giving and receiving trust, in using your intuition (your gut) and bringing soul into what you do, then you can partner with AI instead of competing with it. These aspects of leadership are far from new, but they have probably been overlooked in how we understand our own competence. When we think that what makes us human is our mind, the finer the mind, the finer the person. I have worked in many places where being the smartest in the room was the accolade for which everyone competed, but it wasn't that simple in the military. There, we prized trust and intuition just as highly. Once again, I learnt lessons in leadership from when the stakes were the highest they could be. The military taught me how and when to trust, and how to work with my gut. I want to share those lessons with you. Let's start with trust.

The importance of trust

Trust is one of those potent words that we use, often with deep feeling. To be told that someone trusts you is a serious thing. To be told that they don't is a gut punch. If you take a moment to enquire what you know about trust, you might notice that the answers about how you build it, or lose it, are embodied ones. We talk about a gut instinct, a feeling, a sense – all embodied words.

Have you ever had a moment of losing trust in someone? That sudden realisation that they have misled you? I experience that as a physical sensation: a jolt, a disoriented spin, my stomach dropping away, the surge of adrenaline sending embodied signals through me. Or, on the other side, when building trust, there is the oxytocin that bonds us when we spend time in touch with people we love.

Trust is a deeply embodied experience, but given we're spending some time discussing it, it doesn't hurt to use a couple of ideas to think about it more explicitly. Katherine Hawley came up with a formulation on trust,[40] and I like it. It is about commitment (what someone intends to do) and competence (whether someone has the ability to do it). You need both to be in place to wisely put trust in someone. Someone could have the best intent in the world, but if they don't have the skills to follow through, then you can't trust them to deliver. Someone could also be the most skilled at the thing they have promised to do, but if they don't truly have the intent to turn up for you, then you can't trust them either.

I like this formulation because it allows for the vagaries of life to upset plans without needing to lose trust in someone. If I promise to help you move house and have the skills (strong arms!) and intent (I left on time and packed sandwiches) but I get caught in a traffic jam for three hours, you don't lose trust in me. You might be fairly disappointed, even frustrated, but most people would agree that you could still trust me.

It also shines a light on the importance of the say–do gap as a measure of trust. This is one of those practical tools that we all use to build our ability to assess whether someone is trustworthy. If they say they will do something, do they follow through? The smaller the say–do gap, the more trust you can safely place in them.

How trust can be embodied

We've been using our brains there to set out the equation of trust and explain how to monitor how people are doing against that equation. So far, so thinky. What was I saying about trust being embodied again, and why does that matter if we have this handy equation? It matters because the way in which we establish intent and skills is through a host of embodied engagements and rituals.

Let me tell you about a time that I stood with my second-in-command watching two pilots who were due to sign out a helicopter for a troop-carrying mission in Camp Bastion, Afghanistan. This is usually a fairly swift process, where the pilot looks through the logs for the craft to understand any acceptable faults or limitations with the helicopter at this time. As an engineer, it's my job to assess the helicopter and let them know it is good to fly for this mission. This helicopter was good to go, and we were expecting the usual read-through, swift sign and getting the aircraft on its way.

Today, it was playing out slightly differently. The two confident, experienced pilots I knew were not themselves. They were shuffling the pages of the logs back and forth, taking longer than usual. A small thing, but my flight sergeant and I both noticed, and wordlessly shared the same worry.

I stepped forward and suggested we look at the aircraft together. As we walked to a quieter spot to examine something, I said quietly, 'I don't think you want to take this aircraft out today.' They both mutely shook their heads. They had experienced a rough flight the day before, and I don't think they'd had enough hours to process it.

Watching how they moved – seeing tiny hesitations in people I knew to be swift and confident – set alarm bells ringing. Another flight crew was sent to do the troop movement. Within hours these two were back to their normal operating zone, but knowing the total presence, concentration and split-second judgement required to fly in a combat zone – spotting those small changes in their physical embodiment – allowed us to have the conversation that now wasn't the right moment for them to fly.

This brings me to the importance of physical presence in trust.

Physical presence in trust

In 2008, I deployed alongside the Royal Marines, 3 Commando Brigade in Helmand. To deploy with the Marines, you have to pass additional and gruelling training and fitness tests. Having been injured in officer training, I was determined to prove to myself that I could meet the highest standards of physical fitness and put memories of limitations behind me.

It was life-changing, not because I was the fittest I had ever been or because I was deployed alongside some of the most elite units in the British Forces, but because of the lessons I learnt about how to physically embody trustworthiness and inspire trust in others.

The enduring lesson I took away was that physical presence matters deeply – but not in the sense of how big and strong someone is, how fast and far they can run, or how much they can lift. What the Marines taught me about physical presence was the embodiment of being trustworthy. The Commando Spirit is built on four values:[41]

1. Courage
2. Determination
3. Unselfishness
4. Cheerfulness

These are not the kind of corporate values you find on pastel posters in company lifts. These are a set of shared principles that the Marines mean – and live by.

Cheerfulness

Cheerfulness might not be a value you expect from the Navy's elite fighting forces. It was omnipresent, but not the kind of toxic positivity that insists everything is fine – toxic positivity is brittle. The cheerfulness I learnt with the Marines was the opposite. It was the soul of resilience.

Jokes abounded, and it was essential that you could laugh at yourself. There was a discipline around choosing to lift others up, check in on any colleague who might have a 'sad-on', and taking the sting out of errors and mistakes by laughing about them. You learnt from them – absolutely and seriously – but you weren't shamed by them. Have you tried mixing shame and cheerfulness? It doesn't work; they are oil and water. The Marines chose cheerfulness over shame.

Take a moment to think about how to show cheerfulness. You are probably picturing smiling, seeking eye contact, finding small points of connection when you share stories. Empathy, but a rueful sort that doesn't tolerate rumination. It's a physically powered experience. When a group makes a choice together to be cheerful, they are co-regulating. They are bonding and reinforcing the group.

It is important to place that cheerfulness in context. This isn't Dick Van Dyke in *Mary Poppins* swinging off lamp posts (although I may have seen Marines swinging off lamp posts on nights out!); this is a powerful, physical presence that can own a room. It's a 'nothing to prove, but everything to offer' energy that inspires trust, and they meant it, for they took the other values of courage, determination and unselfishness with deadly seriousness. In a war zone, that means a willingness to put your life literally on the line for those around you.

That way of physically turning up is not a mysterious personality trait. As I came to realise, it is the visible outcome of a nervous system that has been well cared for and well listened to. At the core of this is interoception – the brain's ability to sense, interpret and integrate signals from within the body: heart rate, breath, gut sensations, tension, warmth, fatigue and more. These internal signals are continuously mapped in regions such as the insula and anterior cingulate cortex, forming the basis of emotional experience, self-awareness and homeostatic balance.

When you routinely look after your body through sleep, movement, recovery and nutrition, those signals become cleaner and more predictable. When you practise actually noticing them, rather than overriding or numbing them, your brain gets better at reading and regulating your own state. Presence, in this sense, is simply what it looks like from the outside when someone has a clear, stable channel between body and brain.

This internal clarity is what prevents anxiety from being projected onto everyone else. People with good interoceptive awareness detect the first stirrings of stress in their body – a tightening of the chest, a shift in breathing, a change in muscle tone – and can adjust course before the amygdala runs away with a full-blown threat response. In less-resilient people, those same internal signals don't reach awareness as clearly; instead, they are shunted into the brain's stress circuitry, amplifying defensive reactions, cortisol release and hypervigilance. From the outside, we dread this person's arrival in the room. From the inside, it is simply a body whose signals are not being accurately heard and regulated.

Importantly, mood and response to setbacks are governed by the dynamic between emotion-generating regions like the amygdala and regulatory areas, including the pregenual cingulate and prefrontal cortex. When there is a strong functional link here, cheerfulness in the face of adversity is not denial; it is the outward sign of a system that can mount a strong response and then stand down. Courage is therefore not the absence of bodily fear but the capacity to stay present to intense internal signals without collapsing into avoidance.

Storytelling

Military culture recognises storytelling as foundational to unit cohesion, embedding it in ritual practice. If there were awkward silences, you might hear, 'Spin us a dit then,' and you would have to recall something that would not only entertain but also make the group laugh. You can see why 'Maintenance of Morale' is one of the ten principles of war. The comfort in doing so certainly ranged between people, but I happened to enjoy it.

In staff jobs (where you would be at a desk with a computer most of the time), there would be a 'forced interaction' – it wasn't called that; it was something like 'tea in the atrium', but it wasn't optional. It was built on the 'tea and toast' tradition: scheduled moments around mid-morning where officers from different areas gather, without an agenda, to simply talk. These were important because they weren't about inconveniencing anyone but about deliberate architectures for connection. When someone shares a story about a mutual acquaintance or a shared operation, rapport accelerates. The exchange of narratives becomes the currency through which trust is built across functional boundaries, transforming strangers into comrades who recognise themselves in the other person's story. What might be called a larger ('forced') gathering of 'water cooler moments' in business settings isn't about an exchange of information but a deliberate emotional and moral architecture for connection.

What makes this practice neurobiologically powerful is that storytelling does not merely convey information; it synchronises brains. Princeton research demonstrates that when people listen to the same story, their neural activity becomes aligned – a phenomenon called neural coupling.[42] Before a story begins, listeners' brains show disparate activity patterns; once the narrative unfolds, their neurons begin firing in synchronised patterns that mirror the storyteller's brain. This alignment spreads beyond auditory processing into higher-order regions, including the frontal and parietal cortices – areas responsible for meaning-making, perspective-taking and social cognition. It is not the exact words but the comprehensible narrative arc that allows brains to lock together. The storyteller literally 'herds' listeners' neural activity, bringing dispersed individual perspectives into convergence.

This neural mirroring enables emotional contagion: seeing or hearing about fear, determination or relief triggers corresponding activation in the observer's brain, creating shared emotional experience without direct participation in the event. For military units, this mechanism transforms individual experiences into collective ones. A story of one soldier's courage becomes a visceral, embodied memory for all who hear it, creating emotional bonds that transcend the literal boundaries of who was physically present.

Dr Leong, of the University of Cambridge's Department of Psychology, led a study that found that mothers and babies tend to synchronise their brainwaves – an effect known as interpersonal neural connectivity – particularly in the frequency of 6–9 hertz, the infant alpha range. She concludes that our emotions literally change the way that our brains share information with others; positive emotions help us to communicate in a much more efficient way.[43]

The neurochemical dimension deepens this effect. Storytelling increases oxytocin, a neuropeptide central to trust, empathy and social bonding, to levels higher than other positive social interactions. Oxytocin attenuates stress responses, reduces anxiety and signals to the brain that 'it's safe to approach others', creating the psychological conditions for vulnerability and connection.

When unit members gather to share stories, their bodies are biochemically primed for bonding: cortisol (the stress hormone) decreases, positive emotions increase and the capacity to infer others' internal states – essential for coordinated action under pressure – is enhanced. Critically, oxytocin also promotes conformity to trusted in-group members, facilitating socially reinforced learning through amygdala-frontal-striatal circuitry. In practical terms, this means that stories told by respected leaders or experienced peers shape not just what unit members remember but how they interpret ambiguous situations, what they value and how they behave when no one is watching.

The cumulative effect of repeated storytelling is the creation of collective memory, a shared narrative that structures group identity. Individual memories are malleable; when people discuss the past together, their recollections converge, increasing similarity through conversational synchronisation. In small groups like military squads or platoons, these dyadic and small-group interactions propagate through social networks, creating large-scale alignment around 'what happened' and 'what it meant'. Over time, certain stories crystallise into narrative templates, schematic structures that provide ready-made frameworks for interpreting new experiences. A unit that repeatedly tells stories of perseverance in impossible circumstances develops a template that codes future hardships as temporary and surmountable, shaping not just retrospective memory but prospective imagination and resilience.

Honing your human edge

We may consciously prize the cognitive, but this chapter has explored just a handful of the many ways we operate as complex, embodied leaders – ways that even the farthest reaches of potential AI will not replicate. By honing your human edge, you strengthen your offer in your profession, the offer of your team, and ensure that the human side of the partnership between us and AI can draw on our most sophisticated capabilities.

How do you bring this into your leadership practice?

Let's start with physical presence. The good news is that being a skilled, embodied leader will truly differentiate you and keep you in a job for life. The bad news is that you are going to have to get uncomfortable – not least because being uncomfortable is something that AI can't do.

Think back to the powerful physical presence I experienced with the Marines. The core of that is not physical fitness or strength; it is a well-regulated nervous system and the ability to understand and respond to your own signals. The goal is to be the reassuring presence that provides co-regulation, not the reactive presence that spreads stress.

Your first task is to develop this as a core personal competence, taking it as seriously as you do any other skill in your job. The how will, to some extent, be a personal choice. You might find that the tools that support you best are mindfulness, yoga or deliberate attention to your sleep, nutrition and exercise. The key is that this is not, exactly, about 'well-being' (although that is important, so do look after yourself). It is about getting to know your system. It probably won't be fun, as most of those who have started a yoga or meditation practice know. It's uncomfortable, but becoming familiar with discomfort is almost exactly the point. Leadership will bring you moments of real stress, frustration and the temptation to react. Pick a practice that helps you develop your ability to be with that – to know your own system so well that you can regulate it. From there, you can become the presence that helps regulate the team.

Your second task is to architect connection for your team. Remember the 'tea and toast' rituals from my days in the RAF? That might not be quite the right cultural fit, but you do need to create ways for your team to connect. Honestly, you probably already have some of this in place. Most workplaces are guilty of over-meeting rather than under-meeting, but not using that time to build connection and dialogue. Why not audit the ways in which you bring your teams together – stand-ups, quarterlies, offsites, monthly progress – and explore how to turn even one of these into a forum where you can architect some connection. Ideally, this is in person, and it is to create an opportunity for the group to co-regulate together, to build shared experience and to establish fodder for shared stories and recollections.

This brings me onto the third and final task: time to tell stories. Telling stories together, about your work, has an outrageous wealth of benefits for developing human capacity and shared connection. Paying attention to the formal and informal storytelling you are doing as a team – about your work, your purpose and your mission – isn't just a nice-to-have dusty-management-book idea; it's a bio-hack for bonding. It is the definition of human edge in an AI-integrated world. You can't outsource this one. Because you have to tell them – as a team, with the team – about your shared experience. If that sounds cringy, then step back to task one: get uncomfortable. That is exactly why this task is uniquely human.

Lead by telling stories and encourage others to tell stories of their own. Absolutely spend time talking about the mission, but concentrate on what you need to do to meet your mission challenges and what behaviours and values are required to make that happen, then deliberately pick out and tell the stories that reinforce that.

When you go through significant pieces of work, tell those stories together. If your business is about getting delivery over the line, even in adversity, tell those stories. Create the legends about deliveries that have been difficult, but where you got there in the end. Lift the lessons about the things that people did that made it work, and tell those stories together. Did you go above and beyond as a team? Reminisce. Make it a fond recollection that has meaning.

Perhaps your work is about creativity: tell the stories about the ways in which teams have had their breakthroughs. If you need people to feel comfortable leaning into their quirks so they can be creative, make sure you are telling the stories that celebrate those quirks – and the resulting creativity. Telling stories is about deciding who we are, and then using all that powerful physiology and neurobiology to wire that into your team.

Those three steps will start helping you embed your human edge, preparing you to be a powerful embodied presence alongside a little extra computational help.

EIGHT

Intuition And Judgement

We don't make decisions how we think we make decisions. You probably know this. There are any number of books and articles that explore the link between decision-making and the emotional functions observable in our brains. Perhaps one of the most powerful pieces of evidence comes from people who sustain brain injuries to the parts of their brain we might consider the 'emotional centres'. They struggle with everyday decision-making and learning through rewards.

Neuroscientist Antonio Damasio wrote about a patient who had brain surgery near the areas of the brain associated with emotion-guided decision-making (orbital and lower medial frontal cortices, if you are tracking!). Afterwards, his intellectual reasoning and abstract thinking remained in the superior range, but he no longer turned up in everyday life in the way he had before, unable to meet personal and work responsibilities.[44] It's a startling disruption of how we think about thinking: interfere with the part of the brain that handles emotion, and your ability to make and execute decisions takes a hit.

Prioritising emotions over reasoning

We aren't brains in jars, pickled perfectly in reason. We are systems blending all sorts of cues (including how we feel) and turning that into decision and action. In spite of this, we still tend to think that we use pure reason to make decisions, particularly important ones. In Chapter 7, we talked about the impact of Descartes on how we think about the body and the mind. As well as separating us from our bodies, Descartes also helped to separate us from our emotions. We began to develop a sense of the rational mind as the only kind of thinking that was truly worthy.

Have a think about how we talk about the subjects taught in school. Have you ever heard the 'arts' described as 'soft subjects'? I have. The disciplines that deal with emotion and their expression – music, literature, dance and art – don't quite have the intellectual standing of maths and science. We carry a sense that pure reason is the highest kind of thinking, and we become quite sure that that is what we use when making big decisions. Yet it is the *art* of war, not the science of war.

I bet you have a number of experiences where you know that isn't the case. Have you ever been looking for the perfect outfit, for a party, a wedding or an important occasion? You haul armfuls of outfits into slightly-too-small changing rooms and go through them, waiting not for a moment of reason but for something to *feel* right. Somewhere in the pile, you find the garment that fits; the one that makes you pause in front of the mirror. Perhaps you twirl. There – that's it – that's the one.

We don't just do this with dresses or suits. If you have rented or bought a house, you can probably recall the emotions you experienced through the search, then the moment you found your new home. I remember mine vividly: stepping through the open doorway for a viewing and being drawn towards the most astonishing view through a huge picture window. I felt a thump to my heart. This was it. This was home. Was it rational? I convinced myself it was (the drive to the train station was sensible, the local amenities excellent), but if I am being absolutely honest, I bought that house because my heart jumped with recognition when I saw that view. When I later found out that the door had been open because it sticks, that there were no windowsills anywhere in the house (really!) and that the roof leaked when the wind blew a certain way, I genuinely didn't question my decision. I bought the house with my heart and it was the right, irrational choice (it has worked out very well for both me and the local tradespeople!).

You will have felt it the other way too – when something feels off. The house that you don't choose to buy, despite the school catchment area. The job you turn down, although on paper it is exactly the next right move. We have a sense of the right decision that sits quite apart from how we think we make rational choices. It is not about compute; it is about connection to our own interior sensors, and what they are telling us about the external world.

AI doesn't think; it computes

This is understood inside out in the military, where we train for the highest stakes, so we can't indulge in the luxury of the illusion that we think rationally. Our commanders and trainers understand that when you make split-second decisions, you aren't consciously computing the correct course of action. They build training programmes where we drill and drill and drill. We aren't just building our muscle memory (although that is critical), we are honing our ability to observe, decide and act in a single moment, learning to interpret the complex physiological input that can guide us to good decisions, if it is trained and listened to.

This is a staggeringly different prospect from AI. We have made rationality the highest form of human intelligence (even though we don't actually think that way), and we believe AI, with its supreme computational ability, to be an incredible version of this highest form of intelligence, and so we imagine that it thinks.

AI is a phenomenal tool, but it doesn't think; it computes. In imagining that it thinks and can make genuine decisions, we are not only falling into a thinking trap, we are cementing our own misunderstanding of how we think and make decisions. Just as we are beginning, through science, to understand the things we have long known through experience, our approach to understanding AI also risks leading us up a poor garden path to conclusions that take us further away from the truth of what makes humans remarkable and effective.

If we don't understand that, then we cannot continue to develop the remarkable humans that we need to partner with AI. That is a problem in all sorts of ways, but one of the fastest spaces in which we will see it is in the workplace. It is imperative to truly understand how we make decisions: how it works in your professional context and how you can continue to develop it in staff who are growing up with AI and will partner with it in your workplace. Those who attend to this most swiftly will have the competitive advantage.

Trusting your intuition

To underline the full sense of embodied decision-making, I want to share another story from my time in the RAF. I spoke earlier about the training and exercising processes that go into preparing a soldier for operations. They are carefully honed to prepare you for the most critical moments and the most critical decisions, and I found myself in that moment in Lashkar Gah. We were on patrol, on our way to an outpost to visit the small number of soldiers based there and to resupply them. Patrolling in Afghanistan was a deeply dangerous task. Like always, there were risks of improvised explosive devices and coming under fire.

That morning, I was providing top cover. This meant standing through the top of an armoured Land Rover, manning the machine gun that was used to protect the convoy. It's an exposed position – not only because of the physical vulnerability but also because the choices and reactions you make will determine the safety, or otherwise, of the patrol.

It was a cold, bright, calm day. My body armour fit badly (it was designed for men). We were moving along the main thoroughfare through a village. I was scanning, looking for anything out of the ordinary, alert and aware of everything that was going on, looking left, right, up and down to ensure the convoy was safe from threats. I held in my mind the intelligence brief we had been given before leaving for patrol, where any particular threats we might face were laid out. That morning, as I manned the gun in my badly fitting body armour, I had in mind a particular threat highlighted in the pre-patrol intelligence briefing: a potential suicide bomber – a man on a red motorbike.

As I completed another scan, my eyes lit on a man coming toward the patrol on a red motorbike. I physically felt my heart thump forwards in my chest and the world seemed to go silent. My focus narrowed in, and the world became me, my gun and the man on the motorbike. I was trying to assess whether this man was the threat our intelligence alerted me to or just an innocent civilian on a motorbike which was unlucky enough to be red. I had to make the split-second decision to shoot or not to shoot. At least one life hung in the balance, his if I shot – and many more if I didn't shoot and got it wrong.

I had a visceral sensation, running from my stomach and my heart to my head, to not shoot. It wasn't logic; it was a decision, made for me, for my patrol and for that man. He rode by, going who knows where, with no ill intent. Sound came rushing back in. My heart rattled in my chest, and without ceasing attention for a moment, I continued to scan for threats to that patrol.

Reflecting back, I have a greater understanding of what contributed to that decision. It was a total immersion in a busy environment, with my body, my mind and my system honed to take in information, process it far faster than conscious thought would allow and make a choice. There was nothing in the environment that would have pointed to this being the red motorbike rider who posed a threat to my men. The village was an ordinary scene. Just as the birds singing in the woods signal to their fellow creatures that there is no predator hunting, the village scene helped me to assess that there was no nefarious intent from that rider. The environment was signalling all sorts of things to me: the noise of the market, the movement pattern of the men and women going about their errands, a felt sense of the atmosphere that told me that I was not in a dangerous position.

This was not a computational exercise, where I scanned for the red motorbike that was a threat and fired, as an AI might have done. This was a deeply embodied duty that balanced a risky decision and drew upon every embodied sense and prior experience to guide me.

Finely honed intuition and judgement are imperative in operational theatres, and our training was ultimately all about fine-tuning this. Was the aircraft handling the way it normally would? Was my colleague responding as they normally did? Did this village's pattern of life feel different? When you receive the intelligence brief prior to going on a patrol that there is a suicide bomber threat, you have to trust your intuition.

Recognising authenticity: The uncanny feeling

Bringing both of our topics – AI and intuition – together, you have probably had an intuition about something created by AI. Perhaps it was something you read, or an image or video where something felt slightly off. This may disappear in time, but at the moment the content created by AI can still trigger your intuition: your finely honed sense, built through a lifetime of reading and viewing, as to what looks right.

We might even use the word 'uncanny' for the unsettling feeling we get when watching a deepfake, or reading something that seems genuine but where something doesn't sit right. I am deliberately choosing uncanny, as for me the word echoes the idea that we know that something purporting to be of human origin isn't. That theme is central to this book: there is a difference between what is human and what is machine made. At the moment, we still have an intuition about the difference. Our ability to differentiate will probably fade as AI improves and as we become more accustomed to AI material, but it may be important to remember that at first, we found it uncanny.

Another story helps illustrate our ability to differentiate and recognise authenticity. Not mine this time, but from a member of the Special Operations Executive (SOE) in the Second World War: Leo Marks.[45] As the SOE's chief cryptographer, Leo had spent thousands of hours listening to Morse messages sent from agents. He learnt to tell the difference between people messaging from the wrist or from the elbow. The tone, speed and manner of messaging combined to give each agent a unique 'signature'. Although that signature could vary from message to message – depending on the circumstances under which they were messaging and their associated stress levels – the highly attuned ear of the signal masters could tell whether the message truly came from the agent. This mattered. Signals sent to sow disinformation after an agent had been apprehended put lives at risk – potentially catastrophic numbers of lives. They learnt to trust their intuition.

It is unlikely that in your work you will need to provide top cover with a machine gun from a tank, or differentiate the Morse code signature of one operator from another with devastating consequences if you get it wrong, but there is every chance that readers of this book are working in all types of high-stakes environments and employing the skill of intuition on a daily basis. I want you to continue to do that – to maintain and to improve your intuitive abilities and to prize it as something distinct from AI, critical to partnering with it and crucial to tasks that should remain human.

Developing intuition

Surely intuition is innate – it's gut feel – but how can you develop it? It may feel natural, but like every skill we acquire as a human – from walking and talking to composing music or coding – it is learnt. It develops over time and is either nurtured, honed or allowed to atrophy into abeyance.

The single most powerful thing you can do to develop your intuition is to practise the power of paying attention – to notice, to attend. Even pausing on the word offers insight into the practice itself. To attend means both to give your concentration to something and to be present. It comes from the Latin for 'stretching towards'. All of this evokes a sense of presence and concentration; we are not lost in thought or mentally moving on when we pay attention, instead we are present – with the people, with the problem, with the place.

That attention doesn't just allow you to take the measure of a situation; through repetition it lays down the heuristics that will begin to comprise your intuition. Through the deliberate practice of paying attention, you allow yourself to be immersed in the embodied human experience – taking in not just the cognitive facts in front of you but also building a bank of experience that will enable you to make decisions through sensing and intuition that AI cannot come close to touching.

Let's pause on that embodied mechanism for a moment. As you go through your day, you are ingesting a staggering amount of information and experience. You are probably conscious of only a tiny proportion of it. You might recall the critical points of a meeting or some crucial numbers from a spreadsheet, but you have been immersed in an embodied experience. Everything – from the temperature of a room, to the pheromones of a colleague, to the mirror neurones firing in response to your boss – has been shaping your day. That is the indescribably rich territory of the human experience. You will be building up patterns and understandings, day in, day out, about how that works.

How well we do this – how much we hone our understanding and attention to this process – is a choice. There have always been ways to disconnect, to remove ourselves mentally from truly being in contact with our own experience. The digitisation of work and the dominance of online leisure time are stark evolutions that exacerbate this. They don't call it the attention economy for nothing. By investing your attention in your own experience, you will hone your human intuition and make your USP unassailable when it comes to working with (or even competing with) AI.

How to practise the power of paying attention

How do you start to hone this human-only ability? One of the most useful ways I have learnt to think about this skill comes from my psychodynamic training. It's called 'the self as instrument'. This is about learning to listen to and respond to the emotional states and cues you experience, and to understand whether you are generating them or picking them up from another person or group.

Sensing your feelings

Quite often at work, we have a tendency to push through in spite of feeling tired, stressed or irritable. We tend to equate professionalism with consistency, unflappableness and simply getting the work done. As we've explored in this chapter, a wealth of information becomes available if we don't simply gloss over our own emotions, the experiences of others and how we are feeling in relation to one another.

Doing this requires self-knowledge and nuance. To begin with, you have to be consistently tuned into how you are feeling: are you tired, irritable, excited, agitated? Is the cause work, home, hormones, lack of sleep, too much coffee, too few biscuits? This level of noticing takes work and practice. Practices such as mindfulness, journalling or yoga can all help to build your ability to site yourself (and sight yourself!) in your day. You are using yourself – your own sensing – to understand all of this, which is why it is called the self as instrument.

Sensing yourself in relation to others

The next step is to sense yourself in relation to the people around you. Did you bounce into your workshop on Tuesday full of joie de vivre, only for your energy to plummet when Barbara walked in? Were you feeling full of confidence and conviction, only to find yourself wavering when you saw Barry taking the meeting?

The beauty of this is that noticing, in and of itself, is inherently valuable – and may begin to create change. You are starting to notice what you are sensing and to make sense of it, rather than being unconsciously driven by it. You are beginning to understand your own signal in the noise and the patterns it creates.

It can go further. This kind of self-inquiry can help you uncover patterns, stuck ideas and things that are holding you back. One of the key themes of this book is that what makes us human is our interaction and relationship with other humans. It might be that when your mood crashes, Barbara is the cause of it, or that Barry crushes your conviction of your competence. By using yourself as a sensing instrument, you can begin to open up that enquiry: to understand, name and work with that dynamic.

Sensing shifts in energy in the words used

The next step along this path is tuning into the smaller shifts in energy and listening at a different level to the words people use. In business, we are often so oriented towards getting to the solution that we don't pause to explore ideas or comments more deeply. We want to conclude, to decide and to move on. AI will be great at that – swift, definitive and strong at the solo computation of a strategy. If we want to elevate ourselves back to the true human capacity, we have to stay with the felt sense of the self, to listen at another level and to create curiosity where it would be easier to create closure.

When someone leads with an idea or an observation, don't just respond as a cat chases the red dot of a laser. Look instead to the laser pen and ask them why they think that is important. Why was that the thing they wanted to say aloud to the group? Did they use a metaphor? Is there a sense of urgency or concern? Bring it into the room.

You are using your sensing self as the instrument to bring into being conversations that a computer could never draw out.

The beauty of this is that you are creating forms of human interaction that, in today's pressurised world of work, we rarely make time for. If you take the time that AI is saving you and invest it in one another, you may find that you are able to access a level of creativity and teamwork that surprises you. It can only be done by bringing the full range of human experience – from rational thinking to intuition – into deliberate play.

Conclusion

'We are the music makers / And we are the dreamers of dreams', writes Arthur O'Shaughnessy in his poem 'Ode',[46] which waltzes us wonderfully through the paradoxes, crashing highs and crushing lows not merely of being human, but of our great and glorious project of civilisation. It is a riot of understanding, capturing our ceaseless desire to build worlds – and their conception in songs and dreams. It captures a wonderful sense of the human endeavour, and it rhymes – a whimsical human pleasure that delights our ears and our hearts as well as our minds.

I wonder what O'Shaughnessy would make of AI – of our so-called thinking machines. I wonder if he – embodied, spiritual, symbolic thinker – would instantly recognise the error we are making. We have taken the idea of a 'mind' (which in itself is only ever an idea we have held), and decided that it is the best part of being human. Before we had even the faintest insight into the neurophysiology of the brain, we decided that the best thing about our imagined minds was 'pure reason', unsullied by embodiment or emotion.

The wicked which

We see that idea projected now onto AI. Even calling this thin slice of logic creation 'intelligence' is, at best, a bold move, yet we are embedding it into every aspect of our lives as though it were a superintelligence. If you believe that the only critical element of being human is a narrow definition of computational thinking, then you are about to be out-thought and out-classed by machines.

Or – and I hope, having read this book, you are willing to consider this – we could use this moment in human history to correct the dog-leg of thinking we have wandered down, which has reified 'rational thinking' and made machines to do it more quickly than us. We could take this moment to embrace once again the full gamut of the human experience and retire the shallow, cheap idea that a narrow version of thinking represents the best of us.

This choice is urgent. Because technology, AI and our wider digital landscape are beginning to erode our broader capacity for the full, embodied cacophony of being a successful human. This book has explored the ways in which a poorly thought-through integration of AI into our work and domestic lives may strip us of the very capacities that enable our highest human potential: the willingness to sit in discomfort long enough to learn or to heal, or the willingness to slog through the unrelenting monotony needed to master a skill. It is not inevitable that we will be able to continue to do things that AI can't do – unless we pay attention, and design how we want to work with this tool.

I am not an AI naysayer. An array of AI models has revolutionised my efficiency and access to research in my work. Its ability to search and extract the information I need, and to transcribe meetings to capture salient points, is marvellous. It is a technology as disruptive as the stirrup, the plough and the printing press. It will change how we live and how we work, but how it changes *us* is yet to be determined.

Every story needs a Wicked Witch, but this book has a Wicked *Which*: a choice about whether we use AI as a springboard back into our full human selves or whether we begin to atrophy and lose the structural integrity of the self. Ultimately, the choices of individuals will shape this. Your choice matters – for you, for your family, for your work. Who will you be as you respond to that Wicked Which?

Being a steersman

Here is who I am hoping to be: a steersman. It is a term I have borrowed from an academic field called cybernetics – a cross-disciplinary practice that studies systems, drawing on biology, engineering, ecology, economics and more. The name itself means steersman in Ancient Greek, the pilot who stands at the helm of the ship and finds the way through the waters. That is who we need to be as we navigate this moment.

When I picture the steersman, I think of someone with an eye for the weather, the water and the waves, and a hand on the tiller, sensing the unseen – the currents and tides, the rocks and the reefs that are impacting the boat – and anticipating the yet-to-come: the shift in the water or the weather in an hour or a day. Someone connected to what has been, rich in inherited knowledge of the safe passages and the dangerous ones, but not weighed down by it – allowing for the fact that the world shifts as surely as the sands and the tides.

That image gives me something to reach for when I think about how we navigate leadership in a world where AI is emerging. We are rooted in a rich history of what we know, we are reading the shifting tides and we have the skills to navigate new and unknown waters – learning as we steer. The skills of the steersman in this context are exactly the ones we have been exploring in this book: the capacity for connection, for inspiration, for creativity. If we keep them sharp, we can steer ourselves home through changing tides, but if we rely on routes we learnt a long time ago, if we stop paying attention and let our skills grow rusty, then those tides may capsize us.

I have shared so many of my military stories with you. I have focused on them because the military has distilled centuries of understanding about how to build humans who can face death and still operate – and because it helped teach me to become a steersman. Those stories are dispatches from the edge of human experience.

The story I want to share last is a little different. It's not from a hangar, from the dust of Helmand or from inside Bastion. It's a cold morning in Istanbul, drinking hot coffee and looking out over the River Bosphorus. A man I know only by his first name is about to head into Gaziantep, the Syrian refugee camp, but before he goes he urges me to explore the city. I feel ambivalent – and I must look it because he urges me again and this time insists that I visit the Hagia Sophia. I raise my eyebrows quizzically. He does the same, nods with certainty and disappears into the crowd.

With an afternoon stretching before me, I have nothing better to do than follow the enigmatic urging of my colleague. I wrap my coat more tightly around me against the biting cold and wander through this liminal, shifting city, which throws up contrast at every turn. I hurry past tacky tourist shops, and then, startlingly, past the old Roman chariot racing track. I always felt an undercurrent of unease in Istanbul – a polluted, dirty city with a sense of danger. Navigating both the place and the feelings it evoked in me, I found my way to the Hagia Sophia.

I can tell you the facts about the building – built in 360AD by the Eastern Orthodox Church, remaining a church for a thousand years, later becoming a mosque, then a museum, and now a mosque once more – but what I want to convey is the shock of stepping over its threshold, of drawing a startled inhalation as its size, its history and its beauty overwhelmed me. I felt my feet tingle with the knowledge that I was treading where for over two thousand years, people had brought their anger, fear, hope, pleas and prayers. It is an astonishing symbol of the civilisation in which it sits, charting a cartography of history as it changed hands from church to mosque to museum. Heavy with prayer, it has become a sacred place. Whatever my own beliefs, this place was both a symbol and a physical experience. Standing there, awed and uncomfortable, I knew what it was to be fully human.

We are embodied, emotional, spiritual beings, shaped in discomfort. We spend our lives seeking, searching and making. We are – literally and metaphorically – dreamers. Now we stand at a threshold where we can lean into that messy, fractured hard human journey or we can atrophy – put down the things that make us and let a new technology alter us for the worst.

I hope you choose the mess. I hope you choose the courage to sail out, skilled as a steersman, to find your way in a new world.

Next-level embodied leadership

The philosopher Thomas Nagel asked, 'What is it like to be a bat?'[47] He was pointing to the idea that there was a quality – a distinctness – to the experience of being a bat. To physically be able to send sound out into the world and receive it bouncing back, telling you what the world was like, where to fly and how to hunt. Unless you are a bat, you could never truly know how it feels.

There is something that it is like to be a human, and you must be a human to experience it – it is not always easy to lean into. The something that it is like to be a human contains pain, discomfort, messiness, anxiety and a multitude of other emotions. It is this that a machine cannot hope to emulate, and it is this that will give you your edge. In a machine-enabled professional world, being more human is the flex.

Think back to a difficult conversation at work. Try and inhabit that memory for a second. What do you recall? Perhaps your pulse was racing, your heart rate elevated, your breath short and shallow. There were probably effects in your system that were harder to feel but were nonetheless driving your experience – the hormonal shifts as adrenaline and cortisol flooded your body. You may have found this affected your speech, your ability to say exactly what you wanted.

What you won't have been able to feel directly – but which was still happening – is the way your biological system and that of others in the room were communicating. We are familiar with pheromones carrying signals of our stress to the endocrine systems of our colleagues. Now we are beginning to understand that even our brainwaves can synchronise.

Do you remember, in Chapter 8, the idea of the self as instrument? Being so attuned to your own reactions that you are able to diagnose not just your responses, but how you are reading a room? Imagine being able to do that – to listen to your full physical and emotional self, to have the presence the Marines taught us about: bringing the calm of a well-regulated nervous system into a space where others are spreading stress. Imagine you have mastered the willingness to sit in that all-important discomfort and that you can act as an anchor to others. That is you operating as the steersman, bringing yourself and your skills to read the waters of your challenge, attuned to which tide will bring you to shore and which sandbar may strand you. That's something AI can never do, but if you deploy AI wisely and well, it may give you – and your institutions – the space to develop it.

That is next-level leadership. It allows you to create the kind of space that can truly wrestle with business challenges and professional dilemmas and will build teams that can go far beyond what the mere work of algorithms can do. If you can pursue that competency, and develop it for yourself, your team, your company or institution, you can build a plan that integrates the best of AI (algorithmic efficiency) with the absolute best of your human team: the spark of creativity, the power of connection, the possibility of genuinely new thinking that an AI would never generate.

For this is what gives humans the edge; we are conscious beings because we are able to relate to one another beyond language. Life happens in union with other sentient beings. The gentle hum of a lullaby can soothe a baby because the heart and breath co-regulate with the caregiver. The gentle sound of birdsong tells us there are no predators nearby. That's the prize of embodied leadership.

Where does it start?

As we explored in Chapter 8, it starts with noticing. The explosion of mindfulness in the last twenty years points to the power of this simple (but not easy) act. Beginning to bring awareness to your physical reactions, how they impact your mind and how that can create the space for you to pause and make deliberate choices will transform your leadership. It will also put you – and your abilities – beyond the reach of what an AI can do.

If you can be embodied, you are doing two things. First, you are accessing your own physiological store of wisdom. Throughout this book, we have explored the wonder and power of the human being. If you can inhabit your physical as well as your mental existence, you will be able to work with your whole intelligence: intuition, gut feel and the flashes of indescribable creativity that emerge if you are attuned enough to notice it. Second, you are creating a foundation of connection – with your teams and the people you work with. If you are present and embodied, you can work with the systems of everyone in the room, bringing a presence that reassures, connects and synchronises.

Embrace the in-between

For AI, there is no in-between. For us – as humans, as leaders, as creatures – our lives are rich with these in-between spaces. Twice a day, at dawn and dusk, time and place mingle to create an in-between. Every time we step through a doorway, we navigate an in-between (ancient cultures and our own folklore are rich with traditions of doorway magic).

I want to share with you an intriguing and difficult-to-define idea that is very much about the in-between spaces. The name of it is 'the numinous' and it's a sense of meeting something profound, or sacred – perhaps divine, certainly powerful. It's the in-between of our own mundane experience and suddenly touching a sense of something bigger, more profound. You might have felt it when looking at something remarkable, like mountains, or perhaps through music or dance. It is what I felt when I stepped into the Hagia Sophia. Has something made you catch your breath? Have you ever had a sense of both enchantment and awe, bordering on discomfort? That is what the word is trying to capture.

This in-between space is a profoundly human experience, where you sense something beyond. It is precisely this kind of peak human, embodied experience that differentiates us, sharpening and honing our most human capacities. It is also a tool. If you can notice these moments, and stay curious about what they might be pointing to and what you might learn, you will be able to discern things that are far beyond the rapid processing of an AI.

You are cultivating an embodied understanding that allows you to connect with your team, creates the conditions in which you can think together, and may result in those kingfisher moments of inspiration. You are building your ability to be the steersman: to read where the water and the weather meet, making the fine, discerning judgements that only those truly attuned into their environment can make.

When you can stay with that enquiry, what you are exploring is your own character – or essence. While we might have a sense that the core of our identity is fixed, character is far more dynamic than that. Psychology shows us that context is much more powerful than we usually allow for in how we behave. At any given moment, our character is influenced by our history, where we are and what we are feeling. It is more of a process than a fixed state, which means that being able to tune in and explore it can sharpen your ability to be present and effective.

The psychoid and *inge khööslökh*

This too is an in-between space, between the intangible and the physical elements of our experience. Our nervous and endocrine systems will be firing up, but so too are the processes that lie beyond the physical. In my Jungian training, I learnt the word 'psychoid'[48] to explain this – not body, not mind, but something in-between. The stir that arises when something feels moving, powerful or awesome (in the old-fashioned sense of the word). This is the space where your professional practice and leadership are truly open to creativity and inspiration, which in turn become the creativity that can generate competitive edge.

When I was researching this book, I came across something wonderful and startling: the UNESCO (United Nations Educational, Scientific and Cultural Organization) list of intangible cultural heritage that needs to be protected. Reading it is a wonderful way to while away an hour and carries with it a stab of sorrow and longing at the human wealth we are losing. There are so many beautiful things listed: ancient music, forms of knowledge and arts, but one captured for me the magic of the psychoid being put to work.

One of the items on UNESCO's list of intangible cultural heritages is an ancient practice called *inge khööslökh.*[49] It refers to the practice of Mongol herders when they need to coax a camel to accept her calf. Life is hard for these nomadic herders. It truly is life at the edge – of habitable spaces and of a finely balanced search for survival. Every camel and every calf matters, and if a mother rejects her offspring, the finely balanced survival of the group can be at stake, so they have *inge khööslökh.* If a camel has rejected her calf, then at either dawn or dusk (no other time), a singer begins a monotonous song accompanied by gestures and chanting to the music of the horse-head fiddle or flute. The melody brings harmony to both mother and calf – and often, the mother accepts her calf.

Imagine the human treasure of bringing music to an in-between space and being able to coax a camel to accept her calf. Remember the power of a lullaby, and how a mother and baby co-regulate through the shared sound? This is the same – but here we have learnt how to use music to transcend the barriers between species.

This is a profound, embodied experience. Once again, it reminds us that embodiment sits at the heart of what makes us who we are. We are not just minds in meat suits, as the internet would have us believe – with AI being the mind without the inconvenience of the meat suit. We are complex embodied beings, and when we inhabit that space, we are capable of far more than mere minds.

That UNESCO cultural heritage list offers a beautiful question to the world: What needs to be safeguarded from erosion? It also points us towards the idea of safeguarding practices. As I've explored through this book, AI can erode some of our best abilities and forms of knowledge.

Write your own cultural heritage list

For this book's final leadership exercise – I invite you to write your own list of intangible cultural heritage, answering the following questions, profound and personal to you and your work:

- If you were to think about your role, your team, your institution, what would you include?

- What are essential qualities and capabilities that need preserving?
- What safeguarding practices could you put in place to preserve them?

Imagine yourself as the steersman. What intangible knowledge about the water, the weather and the submerged world do you hold? How will you steer yourself through, investing in keeping your irreplaceable human skills sharp, and sharpening them further, against a temptation to atrophy?

The risks are great, but so are the rewards. You must push off from the harbour wall and steer.

Notes

1 M Frayn, *Copenhagen* (Methuen Drama, 1998)
2 B Zeigarnik, 'On finished and unfinished tasks', in WD Ellis (ed.), *A Source Book of Gestalt Psychology* (Kegan Paul, Trench, Trubner & Company, 1938), 300–314, doi:10.1037/11496-025
3 N Kosmyna, E Hauptmann, YT Yuan, et al., 'Your brain on ChatGPT: Accumulation of cognitive debt when using an AI assistant for essay writing task', *arXiv* (10 June 2025), https://arxiv.org/abs/2506.08872, accessed 1 February 2026
4 M Field, 'Using AI makes you stupid, researchers find', *The Telegraph* (17 June 2025), www.telegraph.co.uk/business/2025/06/17/using-ai-makes-you-stupid-researchers-find, accessed 25 June 2026
5 S Melumad and JH Yun, 'Experimental evidence of the effects of large language models versus

web search on depth of learning', *PNAS Nexus* 4/10 (October 2025), https://doi.org/10.1093/pnasnexus/pgaf316

6 Smithsonian Libraries, *Rise of the Machines: Technology comes to life* (no date), https://library.si.edu/exhibition/fantastic-worlds/rise-of-the-machines, accessed 25 March 2026

7 Smithsonian Libraries, *Rise of the Machines: Technology comes to life* (no date), https://library.si.edu/exhibition/fantastic-worlds/rise-of-the-machines, accessed 25 March 2026

8 UK Parliament, *The 1833 Factory Act*, www.parliament.uk/about/living-heritage/transformingsociety/livinglearning/19thcentury/overview/factoryact, accessed 1 July 2026

9 T Berners-Lee, *This Is for Everyone* (Macmillan, 2025)

10 SP Suggate, 'Reading "beats" TV for sparking imaginative thinking, says expert', *University of York News* (27 November 2023), www.york.ac.uk/news-and-events/news/2023/research/reading-beats-tv-for-sparking-imagination, accessed 1 November 2025

11 SP Suggate, 'Does it kill the imagination dead? The effect of film versus reading on mental imagery', *Psychology of Aesthetics, Creativity, and the Arts*, 19/6 (2025), 1526–1538, https://doi.org/10.1037/aca0000651

12 EZ Tronick and AF Gianino, 'Interactive mismatch and repair: Challenges to the coping infant', *Zero to Three*, 6/3 (1986), 1–6

13 S Spielberg, *Indiana Jones and the Last Crusade* (Lucasfilm Ltd, 1989)
14 SW Porges, *The Polyvagal Theory: Neurophysiological foundations of emotions, attachment, communication, and self-regulation* (W. W. Norton & Company, 2011)
15 SF Maier and ME Seligman, 'Learned helplessness: Theory and evidence', *Journal of Experimental Psychology: General*, 105/1 (1976), 3–46, https://doi.org/10.1037/0096-3445.105.1.3
16 W Shakespeare, *Julius Caesar* (Penguin Classics, 2015)
17 DJ Siegel, *The Developing Mind: How relationships and the brain interact to shape who we are* (Guilford Press, 1999)
18 WR Bion, *Experiences in Groups: And other papers* (Tavistock Publications, 1961)
19 WR Bion, 'Theory of thinking', in *Second Thoughts: Selected papers on psycho-analysis* (Heinemann Medical Books, 1967), 110–119
20 L Bakare, 'Government scraps ballet dancer reskilling ad criticised as "crass"', *The Guardian*, 12 October 2020, www.theguardian.com/politics/2020/oct/12/ballet-dancer-could-reskill-with-job-in-cyber-security-suggests-uk-government-ad, accessed 2 February 2026
21 R Mickeviciute, 'Miracle on the Hudson: The remarkable story of US Airways Flight 1549', *Aerotime* (26 August 2023), http://aerotime.aero/articles/miracle-on-the-hudson-us-airways-flight-1549, accessed 26 June 2026

22 M Budzyń, M Romańczyk, M Pisera, et al, 'Endoscopist deskilling risk after exposure to artificial intelligence in colonoscopy: A multicentre observational study', *The Lancet Gastroenterology & Hepatology*, 10 (2025), 850–859, https://doi.org/10.1016/S2468-1253(25)00133-5
23 GA Klein, *Sources of Power: How people make decisions* (MIT Press, 1998)
24 P Egan, 'The virtue of art: Leonardo da Vinci and Renaissance apprenticeship', *Educational Renaissance* (1 October 2022), https://educationalrenaissance.com/2022/10/01/the-virtue-of-art-leonardo-da-vinci-and-renaissance-apprenticeship, accessed 26 June 2026
25 H Coffey, 'Why the adverts trolling us about AI stealing our jobs hit too close to home', *Independent* (1 July 2005), www.independent.co.uk/life-style/ai-steal-jobs-adverts-artisan-tube-b2779571.html, accessed 29 June 2026
26 JM Barrie, *Peter and Wendy* (Hodder & Stoughton, 1911)
27 TE Lawrence, *Seven Pillars of Wisdom: A Triumph* (Jonathan Cape, 1935)
28 Y LeCun, interview in 'Computer scientist Yann LeCun: "Intelligence really is about understanding the world"', *Financial Times* (1 January 2026), www.ft.com/content/e3c4c2f6-4ea7-4adf-b945-e58495f836c2?syn-25a6b1a6=1, accessed 29 June 2026
29 J Panksepp, *Affective Neuroscience: The foundations of human and animal emotions* (Oxford University Press, 1998)

30 Y Lui, S Wu, M Ruan, et al, 'Research: Gen AI makes people more productive—and less motivated', *Harvard Business Review* (13 May 2025), https://hbr.org/2025/05/research-gen-ai-makes-people-more-productive-and-less-motivated, accessed 29 June 2026
31 A Cardillo, 'Assessing the impact of post-conventional leaders', *Journal of Leadership, Accountability and Ethics*, 20/5 (2023), 119–134, https://doi.org/10.33423/jlae.v20i5.6659
32 L Carroll, *Through the Looking Glass: And what Alice found there* (Macmillan, 2015)
33 CG Jung, 'Psychological types', in H. Read et al (eds.), *The Collected Works of C. G. Jung (Vol. 6)* (Princeton University Press, 1971) (Original work published 1921)
34 J Keats, 'To George and Thomas Keats' in *The Letters of John Keats*, 1814–1821 (Vol. 1), HE Rollins (ed.) (Harvard University Press, 1958)
35 WR Bion, *Experiences in Groups: And other papers* (Tavistock Publications, 1961)
36 Ibid
37 WR Bion, 'Attacks on linking', *International Journal of Psychoanalysis*, 40 (1959), 308–31, https://web.english.upenn.edu/~cavitch/pdf-library/Bion_Attacks_on_Linking.pdf, accessed 29 June 2026
38 H Moravec, *Mind Children: The future of robot and human intelligence* (Harvard University Press, 1988)
39 R Descartes, *Meditations on First Philosophy in Focus*, Stanley Tweyman (ed.) (Routledge, 1993)

40 K Hawley, *Trust: A very short introduction* (Oxford University Press, 2012)
41 The Royal Marines Charity, *Our Vision: Mission of the Royal Marines Charity* (Royal Marines Charity, 2026), https://rma-trmc.org/about-us/vision-misson-ethos/, accessed 29 July 2026
42 J Chen, YC Leong, CJ Honey, et al, 'Shared memories reveal shared structure in neural activity across individuals', *Nature Neuroscience*, 20/1 (2017), 115–125, https://doi.org/10.1038/nn.4450
43 L Santamaria and V Leong, 'Mothers' and babies' brains "more in tune" when mother is happy', *University of Cambridge Research News* (7 November 2019), www.cam.ac.uk/research/news/mothers-and-babies-brains-more-in-tune-when-mother-is-happy, accessed 1 June 2026
44 AR Damasio, *Descartes' Error: Emotion, reason, and the human brain* (Putnam, 1994)
45 L Marks, *Between Silk and Cyanide: A code maker's war 1941–1945* (Harper Collins, 1998)
46 AWE O'Shaughnessy, 'Ode', in *Music and Moonlight* (Chatto and Windus, 1874)
47 T Nagel, 'What is it like to be a bat?', *The Philosophical Review*, 83/4 (1974), 435–450, https://doi.org/10.2307/2183914
48 CG Jung, 'On the nature of the psyche', in RFC Hull (Trans.) *The collected works of C. G. Jung* (Vol. 8) (Princeton University Press, 1954), 159–234 (Original work published 1946)
49 UNESCO, 'Coaxing ritual for camels', https://ich.unesco.org/en/USL/coaxing-ritual-for-camels-01061, accessed 25 May 2026

Acknowledgements

I am deeply grateful to Martin, my development editor, for his thoughtful guidance, patience and rigorous support in shaping this book. I also thank Rethink Press for believing in the project and helping to bring it into the world, and Laurence and Julia for their insightful beta reading and generous feedback.

I am grateful to Warwick Business School, where my dissertation became the springboard for this work, and to Heropreneurs for believing in my vision and funding my academic journey.

To the countless inspiring people I have worked with, who continue to affirm the power of collective purpose for a better world, thank you.

To the British Jungian Analytic Association, for opening my mind to the profound potential within each individual, I offer my sincere thanks.

The Author

Katie is an author, speaker, consultant and coach working at a moment when the relationship between humans and technology is being fundamentally renegotiated. Her work centres on a single question: why do organisations – and the people within them – so rarely reach their potential, and what does that mean now that AI is accelerating every pressure they face?

A military background, innovation consulting, and training as a psychoanalytic therapist have given Katie an unusually wide-angled lens: from decisions made under fire, to the boardroom, to the consulting room. She began her career as an RAF officer, was seconded to the Royal Marines and later studied how technology was changing warfare at Cambridge, before taking that thinking into innovation and digital transformation consulting with UK public sector leaders.

Katie founded Yellowrattle Collective to work at the intersection of all three strands: clinically informed, commercially grounded and focused on what AI demands of leaders who must work alongside it. This book draws on military experience and psychoanalytic training to examine what leaders must protect as technology accelerates: the human capacity to feel, think and choose in the moments that most demand it.

She also works with organisations on data and innovation strategy, helping them build conditions in which AI supports human judgement, rather than substitutes for it. The instinct running through all of her work is the same: when technology accelerates, human judgement doesn't matter less – it matters most.

Yellowrattle is a semiparasitic wildflower called a 'meadow maker': it disrupts the dominance of grass so that a wider mix of plants can grow – just as Katie's work helps organisations disrupt entrenched habits so that more diverse ideas, people and futures can take root.

www.mindyourself.ai

yellowrattle.substack.com

@Yellowrattle.collective

facebook.com / Yellowrattle.collective

www.linkedin.com / company / yellowrattle-collective

www.ingramcontent.com/pod-product-compliance
Lightning Source LLC
LaVergne TN
LVHW030725061126
851857LV00019B/2003